DIFFERENTIATED INSTRUCTION

Different Strategies for Different Learners

101 Kid-Tested Strategies

Char Forsten, Jim Grant, and Betty Hollas

Crystal Springs
BOOKS

Peterborough, New Hampshire
1-800-321-0401
www.crystalsprings.com

© 2002 by Crystal Springs Books

Printed in the United States of America

Published by Crystal Springs Books
10 Sharon Road
PO Box 500
Peterborough, NH 03458
1-800-321-0401
www.crystalsprings.com
www.sde.com

09 08 07 06 05   5 6 7 8 9

Publisher Cataloging-in-Publication Data (U. S.)

Forsten, Char, 1948-
    Differentiated instruction : different strategies for different learners /
written by Char Forsten ; Jim Grant ; Betty Hollas.—1st ed.
    [160] p. :   ill. ;   cm.
    Includes bibliographical references.
    Summary : 101 strategies for classroom management, community
    management, teacher's toolbox, literacy, math and assessment.
    ISBN 1-884548-42-3
    1. Learning — Study and teaching. 2. Teaching. 3. Learning
strategies. I. Grant, Jim, 1942-. II. Hollas, Betty, 1948-. III. Title.
371.3 21   2002   CIP
2001099767

Vice President, Merchandise and Publishing: Lorraine Walker
Editor: Cathy Kingery
Publishing Projects Coordinator: Meredith A. Reed O'Donnell
Cover, book design, and production: Jill Shaffer

Acknowledgements

Special thanks to the following educators
for contributing strategies:

Dick Dunning

Gretchen Goodman

Bob Johnson

Contents

Introduction

*If students aren't learning from the way that we teach,
then we need to teach them in the way that they learn.*

This statement embodies the essence of what the authors call *instructional intelligence,* a significant component of which is the practice of differentiating instruction. What does it mean for an educator to differentiate instruction? It means that he/she knows a variety of effective teaching methods, strategies, and materials that work and has the wisdom to know when and with whom to use them.

A dynamic concept, instructional intelligence challenges the "one size fits all" way of thinking. There is no magic program or one best way of teaching, because there is no one standard student profile. All students are different, and we need different strategies for different learners. That's what this book is all about: different pathways to learning.

One aspect of instructional intelligence is *differentiated instruction.* Some excellent books and materials are available on this topic. Carol Ann Tomlinson, widely regarded as the nation's expert, shares the definition, structure, and major ideas in her books and articles. Below is a brief overview of the global strategies associated with differentiated instruction that Carol recommends:

- **Curriculum compacting.** This strategy focuses on student need rather than on textbook structure. It involves assessing students prior to a unit of study to determine what they already know and how well they know it. The teacher then uses the assessment results to make decisions about what the students need to learn.

  For example, a fourth-grade teacher might give a math pretest on multiplication with multi-digit multipliers and find that some students already perform this operation fluently, while others struggle with basic facts. The teacher would base his/her instruction on what the students need, instead of simply covering all pages in the chapter. In other words, some students would require extra study, while others would work through the chapter as is, and still others would work only on a few concepts and then proceed to a higher-level enrichment study.

- **Tiered activities.** These can include lessons, assignments, or both. When there is a wide range of learners in a class and the teacher wants all the students to be grounded in the same fundamental ideas, he/she can use a tiered activity approach. For this strategy, the teacher must first identify the key concepts and skills all students must know at the end of the unit. Then he/she chooses different reading materials or selections and matches them to the students' reading levels. All students read about the same topic; they simply use different materials in the process.

  Teachers can also differentiate assignments. For example, all students write a report on the same topic, but one group writes straightforward expository pieces while another group writes higher-level position papers.

- **Learning centers** answer the question "What are the other students doing while I'm meeting with an individual or a small group?" Centers are areas in the classroom that can serve as "study labs" or designated places that house materials and anchor activities that supplement or enhance the goals of the curriculum. The teacher need not be present for all learning, and exploratory, practice, and extension activities can be readily accessible for students at learning centers. For example, while the teacher meets with a small group for direct instruction on multiplying with one-digit multipliers, some students practice their basic multiplication facts, while still others work on activities that involve higher-level multiplication skills.

- **Flexible grouping.** This strategy involves creating temporary groups for a particular reason based on students' instructional needs and/or interests. They can be skills-based groups, which are created based on skills attainment in math or reading, or they can be interest-based groups, which are created based on student interests in specific areas of a topic.

  For example, when working on a community unit, a teacher might divide the class into groups according to their interests in the different community roles. Instead of all students' studying all community roles, each small group focuses on an in-depth study of one role. A culmination includes each group's presenting its findings to the rest of the class. Everyone learns, and everyone teaches!

- **Mentoring.** The highest level of understanding is obtained from teaching others. When children support, or scaffold, each other, they affirm and verbalize what they know, put the information into a context when they explain it to others, and strengthen their self-esteem by feeling competent.

The goal of this book is to give educators nitty-gritty, specific strategies, materials, and ideas that support the major strategies for differentiated instruction listed above—and make them workable in their classrooms tomorrow. For the past few years, teachers and principals have asked us for a book like this, and we are pleased to share it with you now.

We have written this book in a teacher-friendly fashion—in other words, using common sense and in a "to-the-point" manner. It is divided into sections that offer different strategies for management, community building, teaching tools, literacy, math, and assessment. At the bottom of each page, a street sign identifies the goal of each different pathway. In addition, an Appendix contains reproducible pages that accompany specific strategies.

"Making a Difference Means Making It Different" is the 2002 International Reading Association Conference theme. We applaud and concur, for it supports the theme of this book.

Char Forsten
Jim Grant
Betty Hollas

March 2002

Timing Is Everything

Recalibrate Your Curriculum and Instruction

Cross the midline in the brain

Appropriate time to introduce:
• times/division tables
• begin cursive writing
• begin board copying

Appropriate time to introduce some abstract math concepts

6   **7**   **8**   **9**   **10**

Inappropriate time to introduce:
• greater than/less than (> <)
• missing addends/subtrahends (3+_= 7; 7-_= 3)
• cursive writing (for most students)

Appropriate time to introduce:
• standardized testing from select testing agencies
• long division

EXPLANATION

Some struggling students' difficulties can be traced to the curriculum being inappropriate for the students' age and grade.

Chip Wood's book *Yardsticks* is helpful for recalibrating your curriculum timing and determining at what age and stage in a student's development it is reasonable to expect him/her to learn specific concepts. Abstract concepts taught to concrete learners before they are fully ready serves only to discourage students and frustrate teachers.

Some curriculum concepts that are often introduced or taught at the wrong time in a child's life include greater than/less than, the missing addend/subtrahend, cursive writing, long division, positive/negative integers, left-to-right eye tracking, and required formal reading.

MATERIALS

Yardsticks *by Chip Wood is available from:*
Crystal Springs Books
75 Jaffrey Rd.
P.O. Box 500
Peterborough, NH 03458
Phone: 1-800-321-0401
Internet: www.crystalsprings.com

A DIFFERENT PATHWAY
Appropriately and intelligently match curriculum and instruction to the learning needs of individual students.

1

No Problem!

EXPLANATION

This management idea helps minimize tattling and also assists students to think through problems on their own.

Tell students that unless there is "blood or bones," they are to report any problems using the Problem Report found in the Appendix on page 105. Many students will look at the report and decide it is not that important. Some will begin to fill it out and then realize that it is not that important. A few students will fill out the form and will then think through the conflict resolution on their own.

Younger students can tell the problem to a stuffed animal you have identified as a good listener. You can also ask students to tell their concerns or problems into a tape recorder, which you can listen to later.

Student Problem Report

Filed by: _____
Date: _____

Description of Problem: _____
_____

Location of Problem: _____

Persons Involved: _____

Witnesses: _____

What did the witnesses do? _____

How do you feel about what happened? _____

How do you think the other student feels? _____

List two things you might have done to solve the problem or prevent it from happening:
1. _____
2. _____

What do you think the teacher should do about this problem?
_____

Student signature _____

A DIFFERENT PATHWAY
Manage tattling and promote conflict resolution in the classroom.

2

Front and Center

EXPLANATION

Q: What types of learners prefer sitting toward the back of the classroom?

A: Slower learners, shy students, students with behavior problems, discouraged learners, and students with learning disabilities.

It is easy to understand why some students avoid sitting near the front of the class. This self-protection mode helps them avoid being exposed as potential failures.

Help students understand the advantages by pointing out the benefits. A student seated near the front of the class is:

- in close proximity to better-performing students
- more likely to receive a greater share of the teacher's attention
- able to more easily see the chalkboard/whiteboard
- able to hear much better
- better able to know "what's going on" in the classroom
- less susceptible to being distracted from schoolwork
- more productive and happier with school

Back Row:
The back row usually becomes the seating area for shy kids who try to avoid being called on; also a breeding ground for disruptive students.

Front row:
Students receive the most attention from their teacher when they sit in the front row but may earn the label of "teacher's pet."

Back Row:
The back row is also an area where students may be easily distracted and led astray by friends.

Window and door seats:
Students— even the best students— will become distracted by action and noise coming from outside or in the hallway.

A DIFFERENT PATHWAY
Provide "first-class seating" to high-needs students.

3

Student at Work: Do Not Disturb

EXPLANATION

This strategy helps those students who are easily distracted by classroom stimuli to concentrate on their work.

Secure a 24-inch-high piece of cardboard across the front and around both sides of a student's desk with duct tape. This "private office" will screen out visual distractions that take students with attention problems off-task. To add prestige to this adaptation, attach a sign that says "Private Office" to the piece of cardboard secured to the front of the desk. Ready-made desk carrels are available from teacher stores and teacher-supply catalogs.

Always secure written permission from the parent or guardian before attaching a carrel to a student's desk.

4

A DIFFERENT PATHWAY
Protect a student with attention problems
from classroom distractions.

Manage with Music

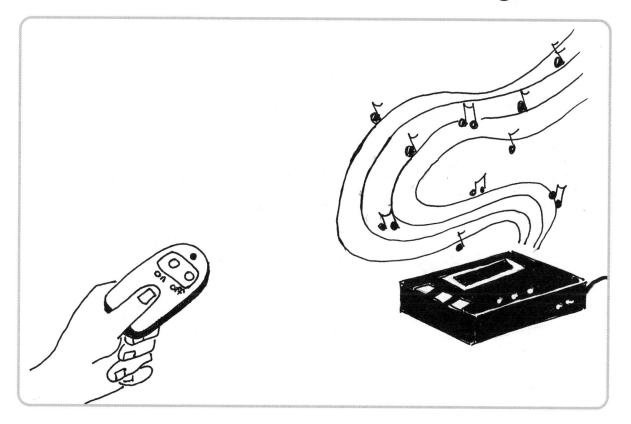

EXPLANATION

Use the power of tranquil music to manage your classroom. Welcome your students to your classroom with brain-friendly background music. Establish the level of your music as the standard for the acceptable noise level in your room. Peaceful music has a calming effect that creates an atmosphere of tranquility.

Music can also be an effective way to transition your students from task to task or from place to place. The length of time the music is played sets the transition time frame. Carry a battery-operated, hand-held, remote-control switch to activate the music source.

MATERIALS

Remote control switches are available from your local electronics store.

Recorded music is available from:
Education Station
125 Jeb Stuart Dr.
Natural Bridge Station, VA 24579
Phone: 1-800-387-4936
Fax: 1-540-591-4199
Internet: www.educationstationva.com

A DIFFERENT PATHWAY
Use music to bring serenity to your classroom and
calmly transition students throughout the day.

Mark with the Sunshine

EXPLANATION

Checking errors with a red marker tends to be a harsh way to focus on a student's mistakes. Try correcting in yellow as a way to celebrate and focus on a student's accomplishments.

Highlighted math examples left uncorrected signal the need for rework. Give students as many opportunities as necessary to produce a perfect paper. Indicate on the back of each paper how many tries the student needed to reach proficiency. This reminder is helpful when recording the student's process, progress, and work habits.

See Appendix, page 106, for the poem "I'd Mark with the Sunshine" by Kalli Dakos.

A DIFFERENT PATHWAY
Allow students repeated opportunities to reach proficiency.

"Lefties" Have Different Needs

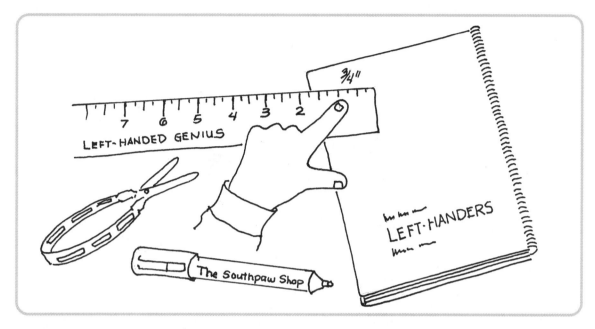

EXPLANATION

Being left-handed in a right-handed world can often be difficult and challenging for some students.

Provide left-handed students with the following:

- A left-handed ruler (no more fingers covering the numbers).
- Pencils/pens for lefties (the wording reads the correct way, and the lead/ink is non-smudge). There are also pens for lefties with ink that dries instantly.
- Special scissors (Squissors).
- Notebooks for lefties (bound on the right; pages are three-hole-punched on the left).

Allow lefties to slant their papers in whichever way is most comfortable for them when writing.

Caution: Never attempt to convert the handedness of a student.

MATERIALS

Teaching supplies and materials are available through the following web sites:

www.thelefthand.com

www.io.com/~cortese/left/southpaw.html

www.anythingleft-handed.co.uk

See the list of factoids for lefties in the Appendix on page 107.

A DIFFERENT PATHWAY
Accommodate the unique needs of left-handed students.

Plotting Homework

EXPLANATION

Establish homework guidelines that are reasonable for students, parents, and teachers. Homework should be relevant and support and expand the student's course of study.

The amount of homework deemed reasonable has been debated for decades. National experts on homework suggest that an appropriate amount of homework is 10 minutes of work multiplied by the student's grade level.

See the Homework Tips reproducible in the Appendix on page 108.

8

A DIFFERENT PATHWAY
Establish helpful homework tips for students and parents.

Listen to Yourself

EXPLANATION

Resiliency is the capacity to withstand adverse circumstances. Positive and procedural self-talk is an important attribute to building this capacity.

Discouraged students and students who have "learned helplessness" often give themselves negative messages that are damaging at best.

Teach students to give themselves a "pep talk" before engaging in a task or difficult situation.

These little messages have a big impact on the student's attitude and well-being. Procedural self-talk helps students remember the steps necessary to do a specific task (e.g., divide, multiply, subtract, check, bring down, and remainder).

Procedural self-talk is helpful for students who have difficulty with task completion.

A DIFFERENT PATHWAY
Enable students to develop an internal support system.

The Eyes Have It!

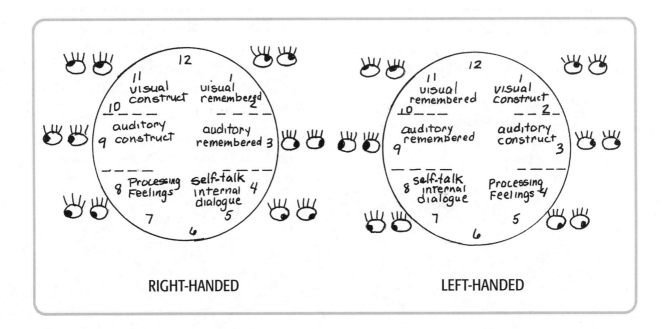

RIGHT-HANDED   LEFT-HANDED

EXPLANATION

Understanding the meaning of where a student's eyes are cast can provide important cues for instruction. For example, if a student is visually processing information, you might ask him/her questions containing words specific to vision (e.g., look, see, visualize).

If a student's eyes indicate auditory processing, questions containing words pertaining to hearing, sounds, and listening would be helpful.

Directionality of the eyes is not an absolute. The illustration on the left is true for right-handed students. The opposite pattern is true for left-handed students.

Because looking upward can activate visualization, students appreciate having informational posters placed on the ceiling and near the top of the classroom walls.

Be sure to check local fire codes before hanging posters.

For further information, see:

Brain Compatible Strategies by Eric Jensen (San Diego, Calif.: The Brain Store, 1998.)

and

A Framework for Understanding Poverty by Ruby Payne (Baytown, Tex.: RFT Publishing, 1998.)

10

A DIFFERENT PATHWAY
Understand how students process information by observing the position of their eyes.

It's a Plan

Individual Adaptation Plan – Form A

Student: _____ Date: _____

Curriculum Modifications

Goal: _____

Progress Review
Date: _____

Modifications: _____

Comments: _____

Implemented by: _____
Title/Role: _____

Goal: _____

Progress Review
Date: _____

Modifications: _____

Comments: _____

Implemented by: _____
Title/Role: _____

Goal: _____

Progress Review
Date: _____

Modifications: _____

Comments: _____

Implemented by: _____
Title/Role: _____

Individual Adaptation Plan – Form B

Student: _____ Date: _____

Instructional Accommodations

Goal: _____

Progress Review
Date: _____

Accommodations: _____

Comments: _____

Implemented by: _____
Title/Role: _____

Goal: _____

Progress Review
Date: _____

Accommodations: _____

Comments: _____

Implemented by: _____
Title/Role: _____

Goal: _____

Accommodations: _____

Implemented by: _____
Title/Role: _____

Individual Adaptation Plan – Form C

Student: _____ Date: _____

Additional Intervention Programs and Services

Goal: _____

Progress Review
Date: _____

Intervention/Programs/Services: _____

Comments: _____

Implemented by: _____
Title/Role: _____

Goal: _____

Progress Review
Date: _____

Intervention/Programs/Services: _____

Comments: _____

Implemented by: _____
Title/Role: _____

Goal: _____

Progress Review
Date: _____

Intervention/Programs/Services: _____

Comments: _____

Implemented by: _____
Title/Role: _____

EXPLANATION

Develop a three-part "road map" to success for your struggling students. The forms in the Appendix on pages 109, 110, and 111 provide you with a reproducible, non-binding, non-legal format to create a step-by-step learning plan. This individualized adaptation plan outlines how you will modify the curriculum as well as any accommodations you will make to the instruction.

Space is also provided on the forms for specifying additional support services needed by the student.

A DIFFERENT PATHWAY
Create an individualized learning plan to ensure the success of struggling learners.

11

"One Piece of the Puzzle" Grouping Method

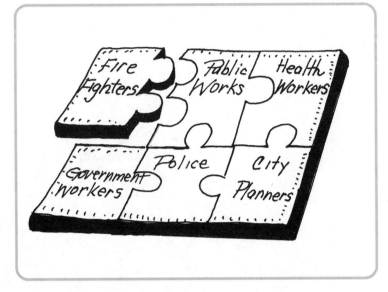

EXPLANATION

This method allows students to work in groups to complete an in-depth study of one aspect of a thematic unit. When student projects are complete, group members present theirs to the entire class.

To begin, decide what part of a study unit is appropriate for puzzle grouping and choose how many topics/groups you will create.

Name the groups according to their topics and then draw a master puzzle on poster board, with the number of pieces matching the number of student groups.

Cut out the puzzle on the poster board and give one piece of the puzzle to each group.

You may also purchase large pre-made puzzle pieces.

Each group researches its topic and then reports to the class by a designated deadline. Group members also label and customize their puzzle piece in preparation for the presentation.

As each group gives its report, it attaches its piece of the puzzle. Groups continue giving their reports until the entire class puzzle is assembled.

For example, your class might be working on a community study. Rather than having all students study all the community roles, divide the class into groups to research the jobs of police, firefighters, health workers, government workers, and public-works employees.

Community Puzzles (pre-made puzzle pieces) are available through:

Crystal Springs Books
75 Jaffrey Road
P.O. Box 500
Peterborough, NH 03458

Phone: 1-800-321-0401
Internet: www.crystalsprings.com

A DIFFERENT PATHWAY
Facilitate in-depth studies through small-group investigations.

Help Wanted

EXPLANATION

This tool helps students signal, without interrupting the teacher or standing in line, that they need assistance.

To make the "Help Wanted" sign, each student takes a sheet of 8½" x 11" paper, holds it landscape-style, and then folds it in half.

The student then prints "Help Wanted" in bold letters on the lower half of the paper.

The next time a student needs help, he/she simply places the sign in front of himself/herself for the teacher or another student to notice and then continues working on the current or alternate assignment.

This is an unobtrusive way to provide individual help in the classroom.

A DIFFERENT PATHWAY
Help students signal when they need assistance.

Manage with Popsicle Sticks

EXPLANATION

Place each student's name on a Popsicle stick or tongue depressor. Keep all the sticks together in a stack.

Use the sticks as a handy reminder to say each student's name every day. This can also be a quick way to select students for group activities. Picking a name from the stack is a good technique to randomly call on students.

When a misbehaving student sees you remove his/her name from the stack, he/she knows he/she must mend his/her ways. That student's goal is to see that the stick with his/her name goes back into the stack. This is an effective non-verbal way to correct a student without a confrontation.

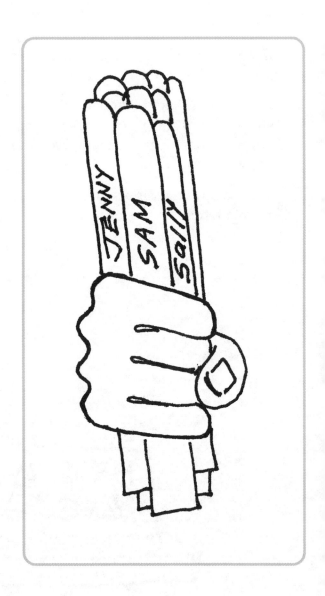

A DIFFERENT PATHWAY
Interact effectively with students in a caring way.

No Can'ts Allowed!

EXPLANATION

This idea helps students focus on what they *can* do instead of what they can't.

Take a tin can and cover it with white Contact paper.

Write the words "I CAN" in bold letters on the side of the can. This is the class's "I CAN" can.

Establish a rule in the classroom that no one is allowed to say "I can't." Tell them they just haven't learned it yet.

When a student is able to perform a new skill or a targeted behavior, instruct him/her to fill out an "I Can" slip.

The "I Can" slip should have a space for students to write their name, date, and a brief description of the skill or behavior that has been attained. You can also use the form in the Appendix of this book (page 112).

Celebrate when the "I CAN" can is filled with success slips! (Teachers can also participate.)

A DIFFERENT PATHWAY
Help students think positively and focus on what they *can* do.

Student to Student

EXPLANATION

Have students find a partner and stand together. You then give an instruction, such as "elbow to elbow." Students are to touch elbows with their partner.

Then give another instruction. For example, you might say "foot to foot." The students no longer touch elbows, but now they touch feet.

After a few directions like the above, you say, "Student to student." Students then quickly find another partner—including you. The student that is left becomes the one to give the instructions.

This game generates laughter, releases some energy when students need a stretch break, and can be used to form pairs for an instructional activity.

A DIFFERENT PATHWAY
Foster active learning breaks.

Stand, Move, Deliver

EXPLANATION

Select any content you want students to process.

Ask students to write for three to five minutes in response to the prompt you give them.

Possible topics might be:

- What has confused you today?

- What have you learned in [fill in subject] today?

- If a new student joined our class tomorrow, what would you tell him/her about what we are studying in math?

After the students finish writing, play some music. Ask the students to stand when they hear the music and move around the room. When the music stops, ask the students to find a partner and share what they wrote (i.e., "deliver" their writing). Continue this for a few rounds until students have had a chance to share with several different partners.

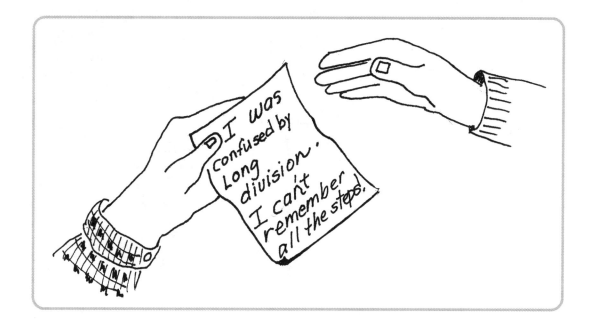

Class Gauntlet

EXPLANATION

Enhance the self-worth and increase the level of security of students who are experiencing a difficult time in their lives.

Ask your class to make a gauntlet by forming two equal lines three feet apart. Have the student who needs a "boost" walk slowly through the gauntlet while classmates express words of encouragement. Give token gifts (e.g., stickers, snacks, pencils, or trinkets). Freely give gentle pats or make other appropriate gestures that show signs of caring.

The student enters the gauntlet "emotionally unsettled" and emerges "emotionally supported."

18

A DIFFERENT PATHWAY
"Close ranks" within a class and demonstrate outward signs of support to those who need it.

Watch Your Tongue

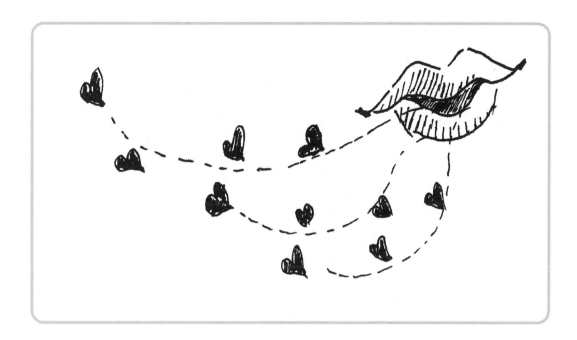

EXPLANATION

What is said and how it is said can have a major impact on how a student learns. Always use kind words and a gentle manner to direct, guide, and correct students.

Negative messages are counterproductive and affect the way the brain processes and stores information.

Make a conscious effort to avoid any messages that might be perceived by students as threatening.

Classroom threats include:
- Embarrassing students
- Giving unrealistic deadlines
- Insensitivity to students whose English is limited
- Bullying/harassment
- Calling on students who don't know the answer
- A suppressive classroom culture
- Punitive discipline
- Unfair comparisons to other students
- Reading aloud (for struggling readers)

A DIFFERENT PATHWAY
Communicate with students in a positive way.

19

Go Wild

EXPLANATION

Brainstorm a list of animals. Make the list no longer than half the number of students in your class— e.g., if you have 20 students, list 10 animals. For each animal, make two name tags in the shape of that animal. On the back of each name tag write that animal's name.

Give a name tag to each student. Students look at the name on their name tag and keep it a secret. When you say "Go," have the students make the appropriate sound for the animal on their name tag. Then each student finds the other student who is making the same sound. Ask each pair to sit, facing one another.

Give each pair the following list of questions:

1. Which animal do you think you are most like and why?

2. Think about your family members and decide which animal each one is like and why.

3. If you had the chance to be any animal in the world for one day, which would you choose and why?

Answering these questions will build a classroom community by helping students express themselves and learn about their teammates.

Celebrate with animal crackers!

A DIFFERENT PATHWAY
An intrapersonal way to learn about yourself and others.

Appreciation Circle

EXPLANATION

Have students form a circle with their arms around each other's waists. Ask them to take small steps to the left as you play slow, reflective music on a CD player. Explain that you will continue to let the music play until a student says, "I appreciate…" Stop the music, and that student then shares an appreciation about another student, the class, or you, the teacher.

When the student is finished, start the music again. Students take small steps to the right until someone else says, "I appreciate…"

Continue this until you think the class is through and then say, "Appreciations going once, going twice…" If no one responds with a final appreciation, thank the class for their comments and give them an appreciation from you.

We are very good at saying things we don't like about someone else. Having students take time to appreciate others helps create a safe and caring classroom community.

A DIFFERENT PATHWAY
Foster appreciation of each student's strengths.

Praise Behind Your Back

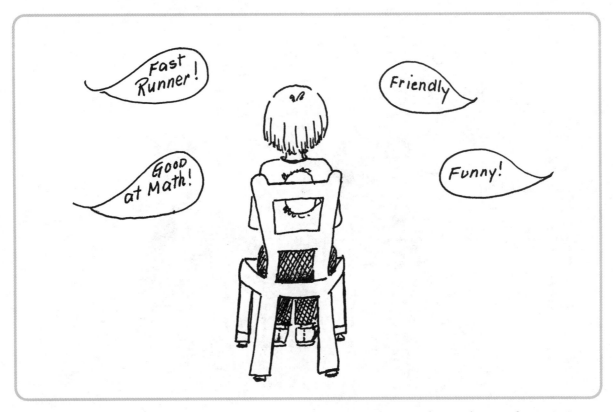

EXPLANATION

Explain to students that a class norm will be that if they talk about someone else behind his/her back, the comments need to be positive. This activity helps them learn this norm.

One student sits in a chair with his/her back to the rest of the class. That student brings paper and a pencil with him/her to the chair.

When you give the signal, the other students in the class have one minute to say positive things about the student sitting in the chair. Meanwhile, that student writes down all the positive things the other students say during the minute. In this way, students talk positively about a classmate behind his/her back.

Keep students' names in a jar and select them randomly, making sure every student has a chance to sit in the chair by the end of the school year.

A DIFFERENT PATHWAY
Establish norms that create positive relationships.

Resident Experts!

EXPLANATION

The purpose of this activity is to create a classroom environment where students seek out each other's help. Each student becomes a class expert who helps classmates with academic or nonacademic tasks. Students design and post business cards to let others know their area of expertise. (See examples below.)

Bring in a variety of business cards to share with the class. Have them identify the purposes of the various cards and notice their unique logos and features.

Give each student a sheet of blank paper and a blank 3" × 5" index card. (Younger students can use a larger-size card.)

Ask students to identify their own strengths in areas such as math, spelling, art, music,

vocabulary, sports, identifying bugs, map reading, and so on. Students take their lists to you to make a final selection.

Once you and the student agree on his/her area of expertise, the student designs and creates a business card that will notify others of how and when he/she can help.

For each of your students think of one or more strengths he/she possesses and create a business card for him/her. In the event a student says to you, "I can't do anything!", hand the student a pre-made card identifying his/her strengths.

The business cards can be posted at centers or stored in folders or photograph albums.

A DIFFERENT PATHWAY
Build community and raise self-esteem by making
each student a resident expert in the class.

Clock Partners

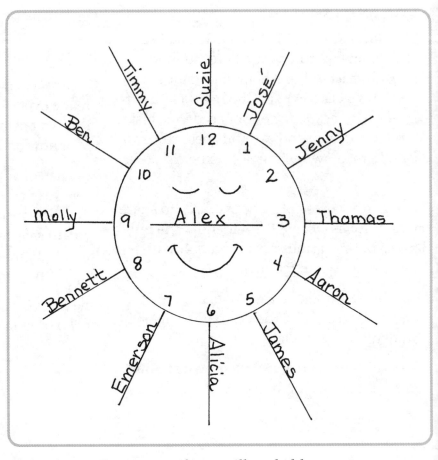

EXPLANATION

Give each student a clock face (see reproducible in the Appendix on page 113). Students put their name on their clock face and then find other students to be their clock partners. They make appointments with a different partner for each hour on the clock face.

Periodically ask students to meet with a clock partner to discuss any content in which students are engaged. For example, ask students to meet with their 10 o'clock partner to discuss a favorite character from a book they are studying.

If you find students are meeting only with their best friends, request they meet with close friends for their first few appointments and meet with students they don't know as well for later appointments.

Because students will probably want their best friends to be their clock partners, make sure some of their clock partners are students they don't know well. This is a way to get your students to interact with students they don't normally interact with.

A DIFFERENT PATHWAY
Expand peer relationships while reinforcing learning.

Mix It, Mix It

EXPLANATION

Students walk around the room saying, "Mix it, mix it."

Tell students that you will say several food names. When they hear one they like, they flock together. Example: As students are walking around, say, "Ice Cream, Apples, Pizza, Chicken." You could also call out a category like "Pizza" and then have students identify different kinds of pizza and group themselves by same pizza toppings (e.g., cheese with pepperoni). Then ask each group to tell the rest of the class what toppings its pizza has.

This activity promotes interaction and cooperation as students get acquainted.

Toothpaste

EXPLANATION

For this activity you need a blank transparency for the overhead projector and a tube of toothpaste. Squeeze a little toothpaste onto the transparency. Ask several students to also squeeze toothpaste onto the transparency. You can walk around the room as you are doing this. You do not need the overhead projector.

Ask a student to put the toothpaste back into the tube. Repeat with several students.

Ask the students, "Would we ever be able to get all the toothpaste back into the tube?"

When students say "No," say, "It is just like that with the words we use with one another. Our words last a long, long time. There will always be a residue. Therefore, we should be careful that our words we use with one another are helpful and not hurtful."

This activity sends a very visual message of the importance of respectful communication.

A DIFFERENT PATHWAY
Build positive relationships to create a respectful community.

We're Going on a Scavenger Hunt!

EXPLANATION

This is a getting-to-know-you activity that helps students identify their interests as they relate to what we know about multiple intelligences.

Photocopy the "Multiple Intelligence Scavenger Hunt" reproducible in the Appendix on page 114.

Give each student a copy. Tell the class that each student is to interview all the other students in the class, asking them to initial every item that relates to them.

When the class is ready, discuss what they have discovered about each other. You might graph the different interests or strengths.

Collect the scavenger-hunt sheets when the activity is finished. The information they contain will help you discover the strengths of all of your students.

A DIFFERENT PATHWAY
Learn about your students' strengths or multiple intelligences.

27

Blindfold

EXPLANATION

Put a blindfold on each student.

After the blindfolds are in place, ask the students to line up according to their height, tallest to shortest, without talking.

Process this activity by asking the following questions:

1. How did you feel while participating in this activity?

2. What did you learn from this activity?

Guide students to the understanding that they needed one another to do this activity. In a caring classroom, we all need one another.

Alternate Activity: Do not use blindfolds. Ask students to line up, without talking, according to the month and day of their birthday.

A DIFFERENT PATHWAY
Build trust to create a caring community.

Flying High with Praise

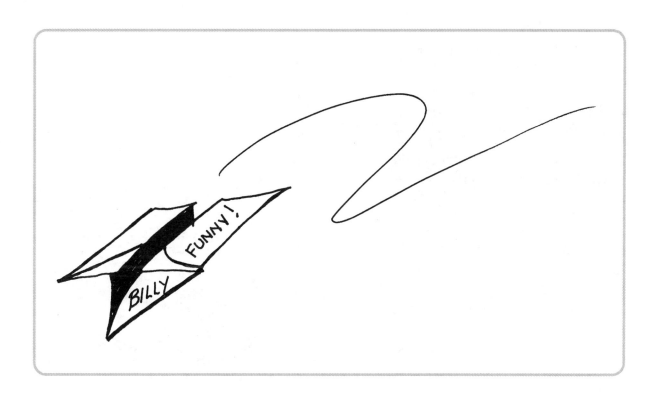

EXPLANATION

Give each student a sheet of paper.

Each student writes his/her name on the paper and folds the paper into an airplane.

Play some music while students fly their papers around the room.

When the music stops, each student picks up the airplane that is closest to him/her and writes a positive comment about the student whose name is on the plane.

Play the music again so the students can send the message to the intended recipient. Give students time to enjoy their messages!

The Classroom Buzz

EXPLANATION

Have students work in pairs. Each partner takes a turn answering the questions on the "Buzz Sheet." (See reproducible in the Appendix on page 115.)

For added fun, have students switch partners for each section of the hand-out.

This quick mixer activity involves students with light questions that can lead to deeper insight. Students have the opportunity to get acquainted and, perhaps, see a different side of their peers. You can replace the "Buzz Sheet" with test questions or have students create their own "Buzz Sheet" items.

A DIFFERENT PATHWAY
Strengthen interpersonal and intrapersonal skills with your students.

The One and Only Me!

EXPLANATION

Give each student paper and a pencil. Tell the students to write an advertisement for someone to replace them. They should list the qualities that they feel are most important. Suggest they include things they like to do; things they don't like to do; a special place they have always wanted to visit; favorite subject, food, sport, color; and so on.

Model this activity for them by writing an advertisement for yourself on the chalkboard or overhead. For example, you might write:

WANTED: Someone to be Mrs. Jones for a day. Must love to teach, especially third graders. Must collect stuffed animals, like to dance, and enjoy reading good books.

After the students write their advertisements, place them all in a paper bag. Have each student pick one and read it aloud to the rest of the class. The class tries to guess who the person is.

Well, I Never!

EXPLANATION

You will need between 15 and 30 pieces of string per student (depending on how long you want the game to last).

Give each student 15 to 30 pieces of string and have them sit in a circle. One person begins by saying, "I have never…" and completing the sentence by saying something he/she has never done. Everyone who has done what the speaker has never done gives the speaker a piece of string. If no one in the circle has done it, the speaker gives each player a piece of string. The "winner" is the one with the most pieces of string.

The game's strategy is for students to say something they have never done but think many of their classmates have done. Example: "I have never been on a soccer team." Since many students have played soccer on a team, the student making this statement would receive many strings.

This fun, get-acquainted game is a great way to establish common interests as well as unique traits among your class. An added benefit is the fact that students must think of strategies to win this game.

A DIFFERENT PATHWAY
Get acquainted through an interactive activity.

Talk to Yourself

EXPLANATION

Students who have difficulty discriminating among different phonemes can be helped with the *Phonics Phone.*

When a student speaks into the Phonics Phone, the sound is immediately repeated back to him/her.

This instant feedback assists the student in making the correct sound as spoken by the teacher or mentor.

Hint: Older students can whisper-read when revising and editing their work.

Directions for Making a Phonics Phone:

You can easily assemble a Phonics Phone by attaching two two-inch-diameter PVC plastic elbows onto a two-inch-diameter PVC plastic coupling. PVC plastic parts are available from most hardware stores.

MATERIALS

Ready-made Phonics Phones are available from:
Crystal Springs Books
75 Jaffrey Rd.
P.O. Box 500
Peterborough, NH 03458
Phone: 1-800-321-0401
Internet: www.crystalsprings.com

A DIFFERENT PATHWAY
Support and provide self-help strategies to students with auditory discrimination difficulties.

33

Twist and Learn with Wikki Stix

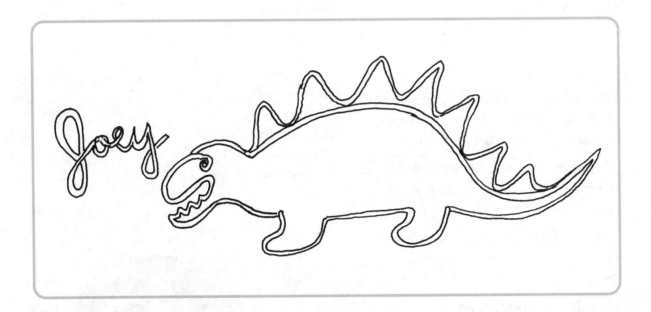

EXPLANATION

Wikki Stix are hands-on teaching tools made from wax. Resembling pieces of colored yarn, they bend into different shapes and easily stick to each other and to other surfaces. They also come apart easily and leave no marks or residue. They are excellent tools for your tactile or kinesthetic learners to use in a variety of ways.

Students can form letters, numbers, and shapes from Wikki Stix.

Art, science, social-studies, and other academic-area projects can be made from Wikki Stix.

They are great materials to have at your learning centers.

MATERIALS

Wikki Stix are available from many teacher-supply stores and from:

Crystal Springs Books
75 Jaffrey Rd.
P.O. Box 500
Peterborough, NH 03458
Phone: 1-800-321-0401
Internet: www.crystalsprings.com

A DIFFERENT PATHWAY
Help kinesthetic learners use manipulatives in their learning.

You Can Count on Bingo Chips!

EXPLANATION

Many math manipulative kits include colored plastic counters. Instead of using these, try using magnetic bingo chips, which can be purchased at most local discount or party stores.

Magnetic bingo chips are transparent, colorful, and have a metal rim.

They are great for use on the overhead projector or by individual students at their seats.

Magnetic wands keep cleanup time easy, efficient, and fun.

See numbers chart reproducible in the Appendix on page 116.

A DIFFERENT PATHWAY
A stimulating way to teach with math manipulatives.

35

Language Pipeline: The Modified Phonics Phone

EXPLANATION

English Language Learners (ELL) benefit greatly from one-on-one direct language instruction. Try using a "language pipeline" to help facilitate this process.

The teacher or mentor student speaks into the funnel, and the ELL hears the correct pronunciation/enunciation. The ELL attempts to replicate what has been heard. This can be repeated until the ELL has mastered the word(s). The advantage of a modified Phonics Phone is that the ELL is immersed in the teacher or mentor student's voice while any distracting classroom sounds are blocked out.

You can easily assemble a modified Phonics Phone by attaching two two-inch-diameter PVC plastic elbows onto a two-inch-diameter PVC plastic coupling. Drill a one-half-inch-diameter hole and plug in a one-half-inch nipple. Attach a four-foot length of plastic tubing to the nipple. Add a plastic funnel to the end of the tube. PVC plastic parts are available from most hardware stores.

A DIFFERENT PATHWAY
Help English Language Learners learn formal English.

Funneling Information

EXPLANATION

Create a "talking tube" similar to the ones used on early ships for communication between decks.

Construction is easy: Simply attach a medium-size plastic funnel to each end of a four-foot-long, one-half-inch-diameter plastic tube. This device allows students to quietly work together without disturbing their neighbors.

This is a great tool for ELL (English Language Learner) students who need the support of a nearby student interpreter.

Vocal Immersion

EXPLANATION

Try vocal immersion: When parallel reading with your students, use an old stethoscope or a nonelectrical-style airplane headphone. Cup the tube end in your hand while directing your voice into the tube as you read.

Extraneous classroom noises are blocked out, and the student hears precision speaking as the teacher reads the passage.

This is a helpful technique for students who have attention problems and for those with difficulty distinguishing sounds.

A DIFFERENT PATHWAY
Bring vocal focus when parallel reading with struggling students/readers.

Mouth-to-Ear Resuscitation: Listen to That Book

EXPLANATION

Recorded books are considered by reading experts as one of the best strategies for boosting the reading performance of below-grade-level, discouraged readers.

Recorded books differ from talking books for the visually impaired due to the manner in which they are recorded. Recorded books have a more appropriate recording pace and tempo, are explicit in giving follow-along instructions, and are accompanied by a copy of the book that has been recorded.

Recorded books can be used by individuals or in a reading group. Each member of the reading group has his/her own copy of the book. When using recorded books in a group setting, provide each member of the group with his/her own headphone. (A multiple headset jack box is required.)

Recorded books make a great permanent, self-sustaining learning center.

MATERIALS

Recorded books, tape recorder, multiple headset jack box, and headphones are available from:

The National Reading Styles Institute
P.O. Box 737
Syosset, NY 11791
Phone: 1-800-331-3117
and
Recorded Books, Inc.
270 Skipjack Road
Prince Frederick, MD 20678
Fax: 1-410-535-5499
Internet: www.recordedbooks.com

A DIFFERENT PATHWAY
Provide auditory support for struggling readers.

Highlighting What's Important!

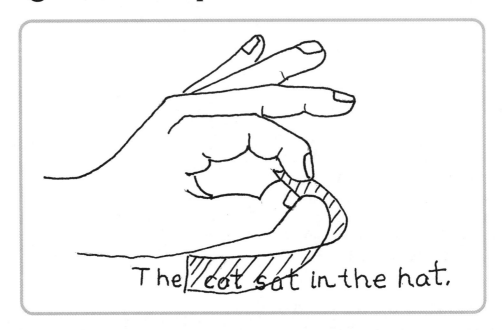

The cot sat in the hat.

EXPLANATION

Highlighting Tape is colored transparent tape that comes in different widths, including full sheets, can be placed over print, and is reusable.

Highlighting Tape helps students find and focus on skills in all academic areas. Young students can use the wide tape during interactive writing and when working with charts. They can also use it to find and highlight letters or words that are the focus of instruction.

Older students can use thin Highlighting Tape in novels to identify parts of speech, new vocabulary words, and answers to comprehension questions.

Highlighting Tape not only helps students focus on learning but is also an excellent alternative form of responding. Students with fine-motor difficulties especially like the opportunity to show what they know by highlighting their answers instead of always writing them on paper.

MATERIALS

Highlighting Tape is available from many teacher-supply stores and from:

Crystal Springs Books
75 Jaffrey Rd.
P.O. Box 500
Peterborough, NH 03458
Phone: 1-800-321-0401
Internet: www.crystalsprings.com

A DIFFERENT PATHWAY
Enable students to find and focus on their responses in writing, reading, and content-area learning.

"Post It" with Notes

EXPLANATION

Post-it Notes are versatile teaching tools that can help students respond to text and focus on specific problems or parts of a page.

As a focusing tool: For students who are overwhelmed with an entire page of math problems, Post-it Notes can be used to focus their attention on the problem at hand. The child surrounds or frames the math problem with Post-it Notes. Also, with an addition problem involving numbers in the hundreds, the student can use a small Post-it Note to cover the hundreds and tens places so he/she can focus on adding the units. Next, the child uncovers the tens place, and finally the hundreds place. This step-by-step process reinforces place value and helps prevent errors.

When responding to text: Post-it Notes are excellent for finding and marking text responses while working individually or in a small or large group. Locating and proving the answer, writing text-to-text or text-to-self notes, and "Guess the Hidden Word" are all additional ways that Post-it Notes can be used in reading.

When revising or editing writing: Students can write revision ideas or editing corrections on Post-it Notes and then put them on their manuscripts for later correction on the computer. Teachers can use Post-it Notes to write notes to students without marking their papers.

Grades or comments can also be written on Post-it Notes and attached at the end of a paper or assignment. There is no permanent mark on the student's work, and privacy is maintained.

A DIFFERENT PATHWAY
Use Post-it Notes as tools for focusing during writing, reading, and math.

41

Can You SPOT the Learning?

EXPLANATION

Small plastic ants or other insects are highly motivational and practical focusing tools. Introduce the class to "Spot" (or another name of your choice) and describe how Spot can help them in their daily work.

"Spot, the focused ant" covers the digits in the tens and hundreds places while the student adds the units. Spot then moves to the left as the student adds the tens, and then the hundreds.

"Spot, the word-finding ant" can also cover parts of speech, vocabulary words, or other one-word responses. Spot is a great cover-up agent for use in "Guess the Covered Word."

"Spot, the world traveler" loves to mark cities or countries on maps.

Students will love to create new jobs and titles for Spot.

Plastic insects can be found at most party stores.

A DIFFERENT PATHWAY
Enable students to use hands-on tools to focus on learning.

Using a Focus Frame to Get the Picture

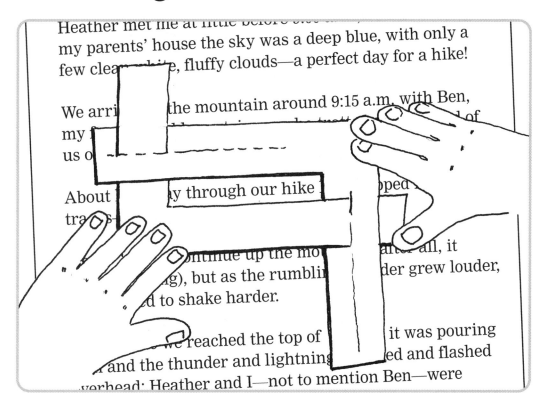

Heather met me at little before 8:00 at
my parents' house the sky was a deep blue, with only a
few clear white, fluffy clouds—a perfect day for a hike!

We arri___ the mountain around 9:15 a.m. with Ben,
my f_____ of
us o____ ____

About ___ay through our hike ____ ____pped
tra___

_____ontinue up the mo___ after all, it
___g), but as the rumbli___der grew louder,
___d to shake harder.

___reached the top of ___ it was pouring
___and the thunder and lightnin___ed and flashed
_verhead: Heather and I—not to mention Ben—were

EXPLANATION

This easy-to-make tool helps students
slide words, sentences, or problems into
focus, eliminating other potentially distracting text or pictures from the student's view.

A pattern for a focus frame is printed in
the Appendix on page 117. Old manila
folders are a great material for making
the frames. (Creating focus frames is a
good task for students to do at a job
center.)

You can make focus frames in a variety of
sizes: small ones for isolating words;
long, horizontal ones for reading sentences; and large square ones for working
on math problems or reading paragraphs.

Focus frames are excellent tools to help
students focus on one item at a time during testing by narrowing the amount of
visual information taken in.

A DIFFERENT PATHWAY
Help students focus on one task at a time—
in both daily work and test-taking situations.

Sliding Mask

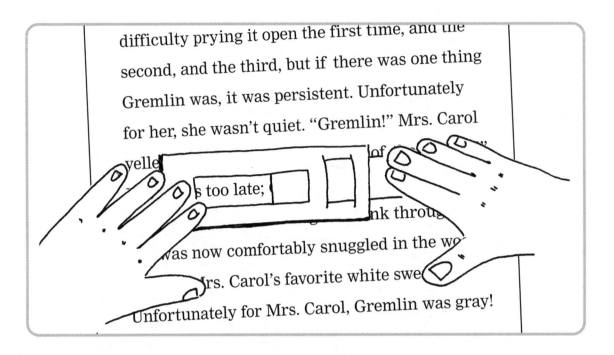

difficulty prying it open the first time, and the second, and the third, but if there was one thing Gremlin was, it was persistent. Unfortunately for her, she wasn't quiet. "Gremlin!" Mrs. Carol yelled... too late; ...nk throu... was now comfortably snuggled in the wo... Mrs. Carol's favorite white swe... Unfortunately for Mrs. Carol, Gremlin was gray!

EXPLANATION

Use a sliding mask to help bring focus to words and phrases by blocking out surrounding print. The sliding mask is a handy device to teach students left-to-right flow while reading or to break down words (i.e., prefixes, suffixes, compound words, syllables, and so on).

Try taping a colored strip of transparent plastic to the back of the window of the sliding mask to help those students who experience visual difficulty with black print on white paper.

See page 118 in the Appendix for directions on how to make this easy-to-use device.

A DIFFERENT PATHWAY
Enable students to focus on numbers, letters, and words.

Point the Finger

EXPLANATION

Use a finger pointer to signal students non-verbally. This is a great way to manage students in a humorous manner without making verbal requests.

The finger pointer is handy for pointing to information on the chalkboard, charts, and white screens without blocking the students' view. This unusual way to get the attention of your students can be enhanced by the addition of a bulb horn or a bicycle bell.

Materials for making a finger pointer are readily available. They include:

- An old glove and stuffing
- Wooden dowel: 36 inches long with a one-half-inch diameter
- Glue/adhesive
- Glitter/jewels for rings and decoration (optional)
- Bulb horn or bicycle bell (optional)

MATERIALS

Ready-made finger pointers are available from:
Crystal Springs Books
75 Jaffrey Rd.
P.O. Box 500
Peterborough, NH 03458
Phone: 1-800-321-0401
Internet: www.crystalsprings.com

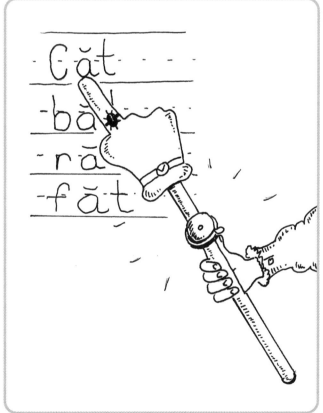

A DIFFERENT PATHWAY
Communicate non-verbally and humorously with students.

45

Catch That Word

EXPLANATION

Take words in and out of context with a word catcher. This simple teaching tool allows teachers or students to isolate and bring focus to a specific word. This is an ideal tool for students with attention problems.

DIRECTIONS for how to make and use a word catcher:

- Glue a 4" to 6" piece of white tagboard or thin plastic to the palm side of an old glove. Turn on the overhead projector and stand to one side, halfway between the screen and the projector. Hold the word catcher between the screen and the beam of light from the overhead projector and move the word catcher back and forth until the word comes into focus.
- The word catcher on your hand will act as a miniature portable screen as you reach out and "snag" a word to bring it out of context to be worked on. This is a great technique to help students who have difficulty focusing.

- When you remove your hand, the word goes back into context.

MATERIALS

- Old glove
- 4" to 6" piece of tagboard or plastic
- Adhesive or glue

Note: A white cutting board can also work well as a word catcher.

A DIFFERENT PATHWAY
Isolate specific words or details for students who have difficulty focusing.

Overhead Tools

EXPLANATION

The overhead projector allows you to demonstrate skills and concepts to a small or large group of students. When you use the overhead projector, you can reinforce student learning through visual and auditory channels. A real advantage is being able to face the students as you work together in the learning process.

Overhead teaching tools are transparent models that match student manipulatives. They can be purchased or teacher-made.

Overhead tools for math can usually be purchased through education publishers' catalogues.

You can purchase everyday items in stores to use on the overhead, including transparent rulers, protractors, and bingo chips.

You can also make your own overhead tools by photocopying the materials onto transparency material (either color or black-and-white) or creating them on your computer and then printing them on your printer. (Always be sure to use the correct type of transparency material recommended for the particular type of computer equipment you are using.)

Just a few examples of overhead tools you can make include playing cards to teach math games; pattern blocks to teach math concepts; word or letter tiles for language arts, and flash cards for spelling or math.

A DIFFERENT PATHWAY
Be interactive while demonstrating new skills and concepts in a small- or large-group setting.

In Praise of Page Protectors

EXPLANATION

Page protectors offer an alternate way of writing answers on worksheets or activity sheets.

Students slide a worksheet or a photocopy of an assignment into a page protector, then write the answers on the acetate with a crayon, a dry-erase marker, or a plastic-tip pen. They can use rags, socks, or tissues to erase and clean up.

Page protectors help save paper, particularly if you do math-fact practice every day. Students can respond, correct, and erase instead of responding, correcting, and then throwing away.

Students love using page protectors as a break from typical paper-and-pencil tasks. After you or the student corrects the page, it is simply erased and ready for use again. The worksheet is stored for future use.

Page protectors at learning centers provide an opportunity for students to work on different activity sheets or portable centers, correct their answers, erase, and return the sheets or centers for another student to use.

A variety of colored page protectors can be helpful for those students who have difficulty with black-on-white contrast.

A DIFFERENT PATHWAY
Enable students to complete worksheets and learning-center activities without pens and pencils.

Get a Grip on It

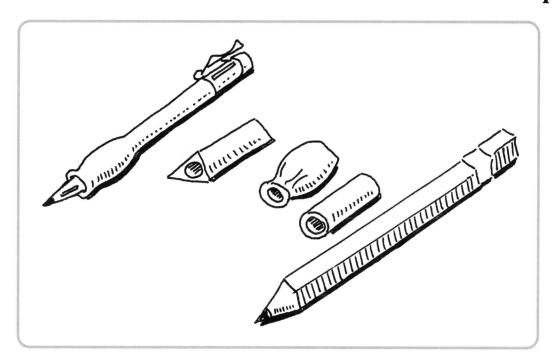

EXPLANATION

Many students have poor handwriting skills due to fine-motor problems caused by incorrect initial instruction. Some students are encouraged to write too early or are forced to write cursively before they are developmentally ready. (We strongly recommend not teaching cursive until students are around eight years old.)

Try using a variety of pencil grips to improve the student's grasp. We suggest form-fitting pens and pencils. Many schools have great success with Hand Huggers, a triangle-shaped pencil that is easily grasped by students with handwriting difficulties. Hand Huggers fit standard classroom pencil sharpeners with adjustable openings. They are also a viable alternative for older students who may resist using a pencil grip.

Handwriting tools are available from most teacher-supply stores.

A DIFFERENT PATHWAY
Enable students to improve poor handwriting skills.

Talking Flash Cards

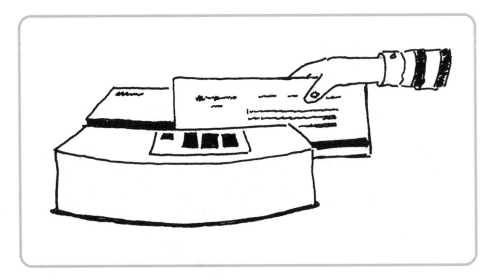

EXPLANATION

Talking flash cards are a stimulating way for students to learn new material or become more proficient in English. They are also great for reinforcing math facts or spelling words.

These unique flash cards have a magnetic encoder strip across the bottom, plus white space for you to write information and/or an accompanying picture or illustration. The cards come in two sizes, one for short messages and one for longer ones. You can order prerecorded cards or make custom recordings on blank cards. Commercially prerecorded cards are available in most subject areas and cover the full range of grades.

Students enjoy the instant feedback they get from talking flash cards. The card is first read by the student and then passed through the recorder. The student instantly hears whether his/her response is correct. If the student makes an error, he/she can pass the card through several times until the material has been correctly learned.

Talking flash cards can be used by individual students or small groups. This teaching tool can make an effective, self-sufficient, permanent learning center.

MATERIALS

Prerecorded blank cards, recorder, multiple headset jack box, and headphones are available from:

The National Reading Styles Institute
P.O. Box 737
Syosset, NY 11791
Phone: 1-800-331-3117

A DIFFERENT PATHWAY
Assist auditory learners.

It's About Time

EXPLANATION

Help students to measure and heed "school time."

Often students from low-income families are not in sync with the time orientation required of the school and workplace. The school is often the only place where a student is taught the importance of "school time" orientation.

Try using three-, four-, and five-minute sand timers as a way to help students visualize time as finite as well as fleeting. Assign students math examples and challenge them to beat the clock as a great way to help students quicken their work pace.

The Teach Timer, used with an overhead projector, helps students conceptualize diminishing time. The timer helps the student complete tasks and projects on time. Understanding finite blocks of time becomes crucial during timed standardized texts.

The hallmarks of time orientation in poverty may include:

- Time is neither measured nor heeded
- Time is thought of only in the present; plans for the future seldom exist
- High absenteeism
- Student is often a late arrival or a no-show
- Difficulty with delaying gratification

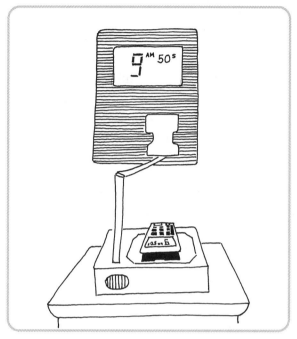

- Projects and tasks are not completed in a timely fashion
- A tendency to be reactive rather than proactive
- Slow work pace

Note: These hallmarks are a pattern; all patterns have exceptions.

MATERIALS

Teach Timers are available from:

Stokes Publishing Company
1292 Reamwood Ave.
Sunnyvale, CA 94089
Phone: 1-800-550-5254
Internet: www.stokesco.com

Sand clocks are available from teacher- and kitchen-supply stores.

A DIFFERENT PATHWAY
Help students with time orientation.

51

Memorize with Mnemonics

EXPLANATION

A mnemonic device is a memory trigger or reminder. Sometimes we make them up on the spot to help us remember items we need at the grocery store. You might repeat the word *cat* while going into the store as a reminder that you need crackers, apples, and tea.

The brain is a meaning-seeking device, so whenever we can attach familiarity through words, acronyms, poems, pictures, or songs, it helps us remember needed information.

Here are some examples of mnemonics:

• Long division: The question "Does McDonald's sell cheeseburgers?" reminds students of the order of steps in the division process: divide, multiply, subtract, check, and bring down. Another example for long division is this list of relatives: dad, mother, sister, cousin, brother.

• Order of operations: "Please excuse my dear Aunt Sally" is a mnemonic many of us learned in algebra or calculator use. It helps us remember to complete operations in this order: parenthesis, exponents, multiplication/division, addition/subtraction.

• Spelling: To remember seven-letter words, sing the spelling to the tune "Twinkle, Twinkle, Little Star." Six-letter words can be practiced to the tune "Happy Birthday."

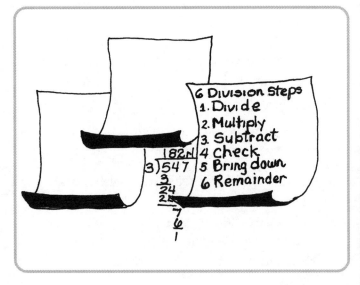

A DIFFERENT PATHWAY
Help students remember what's worth remembering!

Quiet, Please! Student at Work

EXPLANATION

It is not that a student with attention problems can't pay attention; it is that he/she does pay attention—to every sound. That is the student's downfall.

Provide easily distracted students with noise-suppressing ear protection. This will block out extraneous distracting sounds that take them off-task.

MATERIALS

Noise-suppressing ear-protection devices are available from most local hardware stores.

A DIFFERENT PATHWAY
Eliminate auditory distractions for students who are easily distracted.

Enlarge Print and Eliminate Distracting Artwork

EXPLANATION

Use a photocopier to enlarge the print for students who have difficulty focusing when reading small print.

Try eliminating distracting designs and art-work for students who are visually "led astray" by non-essential artwork on a page.

Large print also makes it easier to use Highlighting Tape.

A DIFFERENT PATHWAY
Modify instructional material to make it more visually accessible for struggling learners.

Familiarity Breeds Attempt

EXPLANATION

Pre-teach new or difficult concepts as a strategy to reduce the anxiety and stress often experienced by discouraged learners when new or challenging material or concepts are introduced.

When struggling students are given a preview of things to come, it enhances their confidence while building a can-do attitude. Pre-teaching is also an excellent way to activate prior knowledge, an important first step in engaging learners.

Previews of Coming Attractions

- Capitals
- Spelling
- Grammar
- Punctuation

A DIFFERENT PATHWAY
Reduce the "new-material phobia" sometimes experienced by struggling students.

55

Bring It into Focus

EXPLANATION

When students with Scotopic Sensitivity Syndrome read black print on white paper, the print appears to shake, letters appear reversed, and the print may seem out of focus.

Researchers have found that by placing frosted colored overlays over the print, visual distortions are dramatically reduced.

These high-quality overlays come in eight different colors. Different students seem to benefit from using different colors. (A particular color that works for one student may not work for another.)

Sample test questions include:
- Do you skip words or lines when reading?
- Do you need to take breaks often?
- Do you find it harder to read the longer you read?
- Do you get headaches when you read?
- Do your eyes get red and watery when you read?
- Do you read with your face close to the page?

For more information on helping children with Scotopic Sensitivity Syndrome, contact:

The Irlen Institute
5380 Village Rd.
Long Beach, CA 90808
Phone: 562-496-2550
Internet: www.irlen.com

See the reproducible test for Scotopic Sensitivity Syndrome in the Appendix on page 119.

MATERIALS

Frosted color overlays and Reading by the Colors *by Helen Irlen are available from the Irlen Institute and:*

Crystal Springs Books
75 Jaffrey Rd.
P.O. Box 500
Peterborough, NH 03458
Phone: 1-800-321-0401
Internet: www.crystalsprings.com

RIEADINIG
RIEADINIG
RIEADINIG
READING
RIEADINIG
READING
RIEADINIG

a swift and easy solution for this messy task. I cut an 8-ounce plastic cup (like a yogurt container) to the height of the paint container, filled it with paint, set it inside the paint container, and snap the lid on. Now when the paint runs out, I simply remove the plastic cup inside and throw it away. Then I fill up a new cup with paint and pop it in the container.

No More Clean Up
Having spent countless hours cleaning out paint containers for the painting center, I came up with a swift and easy solution for this messy task. I cut an 8-ounce plastic cup (like a yogurt container or is it a 9-ounce cup like you drink out of?) to the height of the paint container, fill it with paint, set it inside the paint container, and snap the lid on. Now when the paints runs out, I simply remove the

Adapted with permission from *Reading by the Colors* by Helen L. Irlen, Penguin Putnam/Perigee Div. Publishers.

A DIFFERENT PATHWAY
Make reading easier for students with Scotopic Sensitivity Syndrome.

Human Scrabble

EXPLANATION

Make two sets of letters of the alphabet on small squares of paper. Each set (one for each team) should be on a different color of paper.

Divide the class into two teams. Each team member should receive some of the letters to spread out on his/her desk.

Pose a question, such as how to spell a word, a question related to content, etc.

Students look to see if they have a letter contained in the answer. If they do, they pick it up and quickly go the front of the room. The team that has the correct answer first wins.

First Things First: Cross the Midline

EXPLANATION

Some students experience reading and writing difficulty due to an inability to cross the brain's midline (i.e., the body's center meridian).

When reading and/or writing, these students might hesitate or stop in the center of the page. Some students may actually start over again or go to the next line without completing the current line.

The left and right hemispheres often don't interact efficiently until students are around six years of age. This can pose a problem for developmentally young children who are being required to "sweep their eyes" from left to right before they are physiologically ready to do so.

To determine whether your students are able to cross the midline, simply have them reach up over their head and cup and hold the opposite ear. This is a difficult task for those with difficulty crossing the midline. Another test is having students draw a large circle on the chalkboard in one circular motion. If a child moves the chalk from one hand to another halfway through or takes a side step to complete the circle, he/she might have midline problems.

If a child is fully six years old and still experiencing difficulty crossing the midline,

help may be warranted. Occupational therapists suggest the following:

- Have the student draw an imaginary figure eight in the air. Do this eight to ten times with alternate hands.
- Reach across with one hand and touch the opposite thigh or knee. Do this eight to ten times with alternate hands.
- Have the student lift his/her leg, reach back with the opposite hand, and touch the raised heel. Do this six to eight times, alternating hands each time.

A DIFFERENT PATHWAY
Help students who might not be crossing the midline.

Teach in Chunks

Integrate the curriculum!
Get it all in!

EXPLANATION

"Can't see the forest for the trees" is one way to describe the confusion felt by some students who are bewildered by an overly integrated curriculum. When several subjects or concepts are blended together in an integrated format, some students can experience information overload.

These students might learn some concepts best when the concepts are presented in meaningful, bite-size chunks. For these students, learning the parts to the whole makes the most sense.

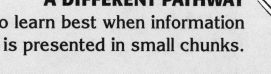

A DIFFERENT PATHWAY
Assist students who learn best when information is presented in small chunks.

59

C.A.P.S. Off to Editing

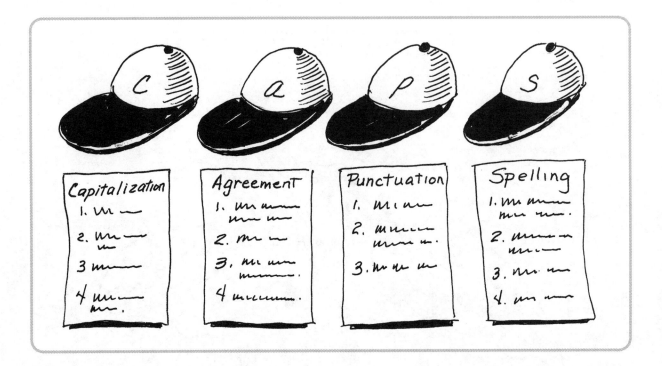

EXPLANATION

This mnemonic management process for editing helps students check their conventions in writing, one step at a time.

Take four different-colored baseball caps and write the first letter of each of the following titles on each of the cap rims: Capitalization, Agreement, Punctuation, and Spelling.

Hang four hooks at your writing center and hang the caps on them.

Make up four checklists for students to easily reference while they edit. Each checklist should have examples of rules for capital letters, subject/verb agreement, punctuation, and spelling that you have studied to date. Laminate the checklists or place them in pocket portfolios, and then hang them on hooks below each appropriate cap.

Explain to students that they are to edit their writing, one skill at a time, beginning with the C for capitalization and continuing until they have spelled C.A.P.S.

A DIFFERENT PATHWAY
Help students use a mnemonic process to edit their writing one step at a time.

4-6-8

EXPLANATION

Have students make three columns on a piece of paper.

Instruct them to number the first column one to four and label it "Characters," number the second column one to six and label it "Settings," and number the third column one to eight and label it "Events."

In the first column, students should list characters from any books they have read. The characters do not all have to be from the same book.

In the second column, students write different settings where a story could take place.

In the last column, students should write eight different events that could happen in a story.

Ask students to circle certain items—their #2 character, their #5 setting, and their #7

event, for example. Students then write a story using their circled character, setting, and event.

Students can share their stories with one another.

You can add novelty to this activity by having students work in groups of three. Give a red dot to one student in each group. Students with red dots think of a character. Give a blue dot to another student in each group. Students with blue dots think of a setting. Give a green dot to the third student in each group. That student thinks of an event. After the students write a story together, have the students with red dots, for example, switch groups.

See the reproducible for 4-6-8 in the Appendix on page 120.

#2   #5   #7

Word Map

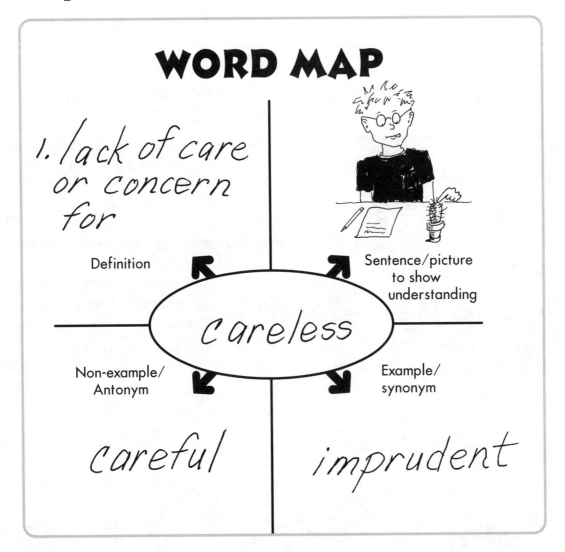

WORD MAP

1. lack of care or concern for

Definition

Sentence/picture to show understanding

careless

Non-example/ Antonym

Example/ synonym

careful

imprudent

EXPLANATION

Divide students into teams.

Give each team a large sheet of paper and some markers.

Assign to each team a different vocabulary word or concept being studied.

Each team should create a Word Map using the reproducible guide in the Appendix on page 121.

Maps can be presented to the rest of the class and hung in the classroom.

A DIFFERENT PATHWAY
Explore new words on many levels and teach deep processing of words.

Three Facts and a Fib

EXPLANATION

Give each student an index card. Ask students to make up four statements about any content they have studied. Three of the statements should be true, and one should be false.

Students then move around the room sharing statements with one another. Students try to pick the false statement on the card. If a student fools another student, the student who was fooled signs the back of the index card of the student who fooled him/her.

After students have returned to their seats, find the one who was able to fool the most students by having students count the number of signatures on the backs of their cards.

A DIFFERENT PATHWAY
Review content through an active hands-on activity.

63

Splash and Sort

EXPLANATION

Words from a reading selection are "splashed" at angles on an overhead before students have read the selection.

In teams, students work to create one or more sentences combining some or all of the words to predict how the words might go together in the text they are about to read.

After the class has read the material, each group can discuss their predictions and modify their statements considering the new information they have.

Another way for students to work with the "splash and sort" strategy is to work in pairs and categorize words about a particular concept the class is about to study.

  **A DIFFERENT PATHWAY**
Make predictions as a prereading strategy.

C.P.S.R. (Copy-Pair-Share-Respond)

EXPLANATION

After students have read from a chapter book or content area, ask them to copy in a writing journal the part they found most interesting. Tell them to copy the sentences clearly so another student can read them.

Students trade journals with a partner.

Each student reads what his/her partner has written and responds in writing to what the partner has written. This back-and-forth "conversation" can last as long as you deem necessary.

Peer response through a silent, written conversation is social and motivational.

See the list of C.P.S.R. Response Starters in the Appendix on page 122. Students can use these if they need support in responding to what their partner has written.

A DIFFERENT PATHWAY
Build opportunities for peer response
during reading and writing.

Apply a Different Symbol System

EXPLANATION

Direct instruction of vocabulary words or concepts should involve more than just looking the words up in the dictionary. For active involvement and deep processing of the words being studied, ask students to do the following:

- Draw the word.
- Act out the word.
- Think of a song title for the word.

Students can find a partner and share their drawings, act out their charades for one another, and share song titles.

When you ask students to draw their vocabulary word, you are tapping into their visual/spatial intelligence. When you ask students to act out their word, you are tapping into their bodily/kinesthetic intelligence. When you ask students to think of a song title, you are tapping into their musical intelligence. The chances of students' remembering the words are greater because of their active involvement.

A DIFFERENT PATHWAY
Use multiple intelligence activities to develop vocabulary.

Colorful Questions

EXPLANATION

Help students remember the categories of questions in Question-Answer-Relationships (Raphael 1982) by color-coding the questions as follows:

- "Right there" questions are green because you can go to the answer in the book/text.
- "Search and find" questions are yellow because you slow down and look in several places for the answer in the book/text.
- "Author and me" questions are red because you stop and look for clues and evidence the author gives you and combine that with what's in your head to figure out the answer.

- "On my own" questions are black because you don't have to read the text to answer these. Just as in race-car driving, black is off the track.

EXAMPLES:

GREEN QUESTIONS	YELLOW QUESTIONS	RED QUESTIONS	BLACK QUESTIONS
Go to the answer.	*Slow down and look for the answer.*	*Stop and look for clues and evidence.*	*Off the track.*
There was a gas shortage, so Charlene rode her bike to work.	Lil went shopping. She bought flowers at the market. Later she went to the hardware store and bought a lock for her luggage. At the pet store she bought a collar for her dog.	In 1782, the Founding Fathers selected the bald eagle as the national bird.	Students are going to begin a two-week unit on friendship. Before the unit starts, the teacher asks:
What did Charlene ride to work?	*What did Lil buy on her shopping trip?*	*Name some of the men who might have been voting on the national bird in 1782.*	*What are the qualities of a good friend?*

A DIFFERENT PATHWAY
Learn different types of questions through color-coding.

67

Over the Head

EXPLANATION

Put each of the vocabulary words being studied from a unit on sentence strips, with one word on each strip. Staple the strips to make headbands.

Distribute the headbands, instructing the students to each put one on without looking at the word on their headband.

When all students have a headband on, they get up and move around the room, asking each other questions about the vocabulary word on their head in an attempt to guess the word. Sample questions might be "What is a synonym for me (the word written on the headband)?" or "What is an essential characteristic of me?"

Give students enough time so that they can figure out their word. Students enjoy the active involvement of this strategy.

A DIFFERENT PATHWAY
An interactive group or partner activity to build vocabulary.

Partner Pair

EXPLANATION

Pair your students as close as possible by readability and fluency levels.

During "Partner Pair," students sit with their partner. Each has a copy of the same reading book.

Partner A reads aloud for five minutes to Partner B. Partner B then must para-phrase for Partner A what the section that Partner A read was about.

Students then switch roles. To ensure fluency practice, Partner B rereads the last two pages that Partner A read. Repeated readings help build fluency.

Students can keep their own records.

A DIFFERENT PATHWAY
Build fluency and comprehension through partner-pairing.

69

Pass It On

EXPLANATION

Select a variety of books for students to examine for future independent reading.

Divide students into groups. Give each group a recording form that has a place to write the book title and comments.

Each student selects a book, examines it, and then fills out the recording form, writing the title and a few brief comments.

After three minutes, students rotate the books to the right, and the process begins again.

At the end of the cycle, each student has examined each book.

Have students put a star next to the titles of the ones they might want to read during independent reading time.

A DIFFERENT PATHWAY
Encourage independent reading through pass-alongs.

Sticky-Note Symbols

EXPLANATION

Before students begin reading a passage of text, provide them with a supply of Post-it Notes that they can use to record their responses. Use symbols to help students code the text. The coding might include the following symbols:

! means *This is interesting.*

? means *I am confused.*

• means *I already know this.*

Students should place the Post-it Notes in the text as they respond to what they are reading.

When students are finished reading, they can discuss their Post-it Note markings and their understanding of the passage with a partner.

This strategy helps students focus and think while they are reading.

A DIFFERENT PATHWAY
Engage and respond to text through Post-it Notes.

71

Team Windowpane Discussion

EXPLANATION

This strategy gives students the opportunity to visualize, create a nonlinguistic representation, and collaborate in the learning process.

Ask students to put their heads down on their desks and close their eyes. Read to them from a book. As you read, tell them what you are seeing in your mind as you are reading. Ask them to see in their minds what they hear you say.

Keep reading from the selected text as you ask students to see pictures in their minds of what you are reading. Ask them to tell you what they see.

Students work independently to draw pictures of their favorite scenes that they see in their minds. *Windowpaning* refers to the drawings the students make of their favorite scenes. Students can share their drawings in small groups.

A DIFFERENT PATHWAY
Create visual representations of learning.

Magic 20

EXPLANATION

Select a writing passage three to five paragraphs long.

Place the passage on the overhead and cover all the paragraphs except the first one.

Have students read the paragraph and then cover it.

Ask students to write a summary from recall in 20 words or less.

Repeat this process with the remaining paragraphs.

When the students have summarized all the paragraphs, ask them to combine the summaries of each, in sequential order, until they have one final summary of 20 words.

A DIFFERENT PATHWAY
Summarize and sequence passages through a group activity.

73

One Strip at a Time

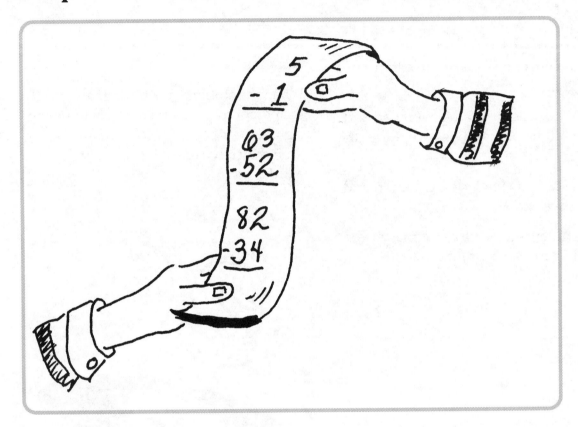

EXPLANATION

Cut math papers into strips. Encourage your discouraged learners to do one strip at a time. Correct each strip as they are completed. This will limit the number of possible mistakes a student can make per paper.

Try cutting the strips vertically as a way to vary the level of difficulty.

A DIFFERENT PATHWAY
Tailor the math workload of discouraged students.

Go to the Mat for Learning

EXPLANATION

Provide students with a variety of reusable plastic place mats and a water-soluble marker.

Mat work is ideal for practicing and achieving success with math facts. This is also a worthwhile activity for students to work on during transitions from one subject/activity to another.

This practice activity is fun and can be worked on whenever students have a few free moments.

Post a sign in your classroom that says "Practice Makes Permanent."

Mats are available in most education stores.

A DIFFERENT PATHWAY
Enable students to practice and achieve success with math facts.

75

Teach with Edibles

EXPLANATION

Teaching math concepts with edibles is a motivational technique that is not only exciting but delicious, too. This technique rewards students by allowing them to "eat the answers." Students should be taught appropriate precautions to take before handling food.

Favorite edibles include jelly beans, plain M&Ms, Cheerios, Wheat Chex, and Skit-

tles. A 12-segment Hershey chocolate bar is a tasty tool for teaching fractions.

Caution: Teachers should carefully read labels to avoid products that contain peanuts, which can be harmful or even fatal to some students.

See pages 123–124 in the Appendix for a food allergy form reproducible.

A DIFFERENT PATHWAY
Motivate students to learn math concepts.

Skill Levels Students Can Deal With

EXPLANATION

This is not an activity, but rather a great way to presort playing cards to match the skills of a wide level of learners in your classroom. Then, when students play math games, you have put a "skill-level ceiling" on the materials for their practice.

Remove the face cards and aces from several decks of playing cards. (You can use the aces for 1's.)

Divide the rest of the cards into piles of 2's, 3's, 4's, and so on, through 10's.

Create pre-leveled addition decks that make the following:
- sums through 6 (use cards: 2 and 3)
- sums through 8 (use cards: 2, 3, and 4)

And so on, up to:
- sums through 20 (use cards: 2, 3, 4, 5, 6, 7, 8, 9, and 10)

Also create pre-leveled decks that allow students to practice their multiplication facts. The addends cannot exceed the target sum.

Note: Casinos use cards once, punch a hole in them, and then discard them. Send a letter written on your school stationery to a casino to request these once-used cards for your classroom.

A DIFFERENT PATHWAY
Level playing cards for specific, targeted math-fact practice.

77

Projecting Calculations Everyone Can See

EXPLANATION

An overhead calculator is a highly effective tool to use with a small or large group of students. It enables you to demonstrate and interact with students as they learn the different functions of calculators.

Texas Instruments makes a variety of models of overhead calculators that are companions to student hand-held ones. The *TI108* is a less expensive and basic model. *The Educator* is the ideal tool for the intermediate classroom.

The Educator is a particularly remarkable calculator. It computes fractions and decimals and converts one to the other. It also rounds decimal numbers to the closest whole number. There is a key for students to compute integer division, so the answer on the display appears as a quotient and remainder.

For information on overhead calculators, check your math series catalog or an electronics warehouse. (Check with your school secretary for a reliable one to contact.) Texas Instruments can be accessed at the following web site:

www.education.ti.com

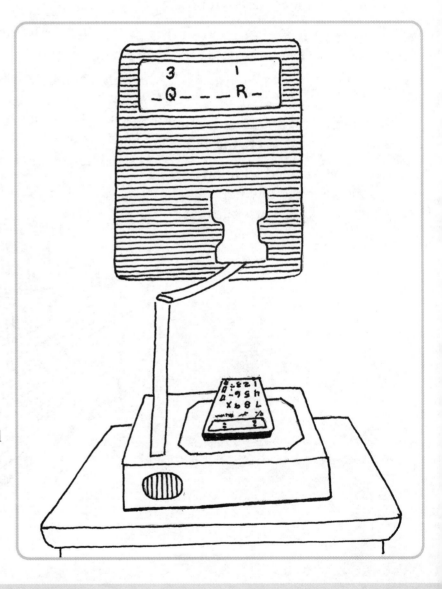

A DIFFERENT PATHWAY
Work interactively with students using calculators to do math in small- or large-group situations.

Capture Math Facts with Captive Dice

EXPLANATION

This is not an activity, but rather a quick and easy way to level and store dice for students to use when practicing their math facts.

Get small transparent food containers with snap-on lids.

Place a pair of dice or number cubes in each container.

Snap on the lid, and you have captive dice for students to practice their math facts.

Superglue those lids so you never lose the dice!

Note: For the multi-ability classroom, use combinations of other polyhedral dice in the containers. Examples include the following:

- octahedron: eight-sided solid (sums of 16; products of 64)
- dodecahedron: twelve-sided solid (sums of 24; products of 144)
- icosahedron: twenty-sided solid (sums of 40; products of 400)

Dice are available from your local teacher supply store.

A DIFFERENT PATHWAY
Store and level math manipulatives for practicing math facts.

I've Got Time!

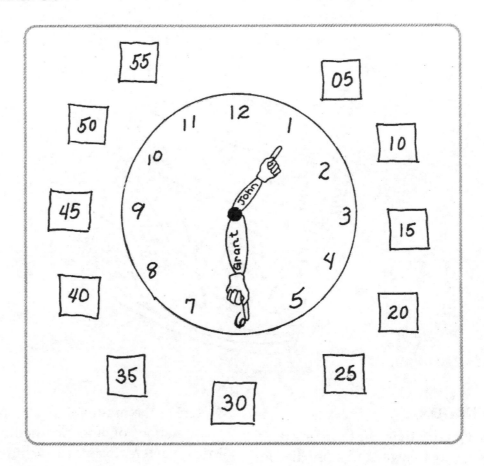

EXPLANATION

This simple idea helps students tell time to the closest five-minute interval on an analog clock.

Take eleven 3" × 5" index cards. Write a multiple of 5 (from 5 to 55) in bold print on each card. Attach the cards to the wall next to the clock as shown in the above illustration.

Ask students to tell the time frequently throughout the day.

In her book *I Can Learn!*, Gretchen Goodman offers the following helpful idea: Write a student's first name on the hour hand and last name on the minute hand. This helps them remember the order in which to tell time (e.g.: John [hour] Grant [minute] = 1:27.)

A DIFFERENT PATHWAY
Help students tell time to the closest five-minute interval.

Triangular Number Bonds

EXPLANATION

Triangular flash cards reinforce number-family relationships for both addition/subtraction and multiplication/division facts.

You can make your own overhead examples to use with students by cutting out triangles from clear transparency material or clear book-report covers and then writing fact families on the sheets. (See the illustration below.)

If you have a job center or students who like to be helpers, they can cut out triangles from old manila folders. A variety of number families can be written on the flash cards, which are then placed in the math center for use.

Triangular flash cards are also published by Trend Enterprises Inc. and are available at teacher stores, through teacher-supply catalogues, and at some office-supply stores. You can also try going to the Trend web site at: www.trendenterprises.com.

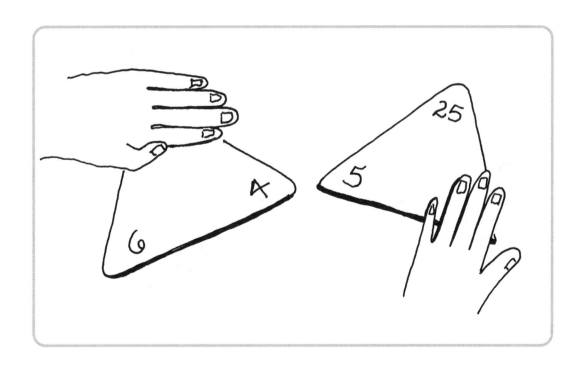

A DIFFERENT PATHWAY
Reinforce students' understanding of, and skills with, number families.

81

This Ruler Measures Up

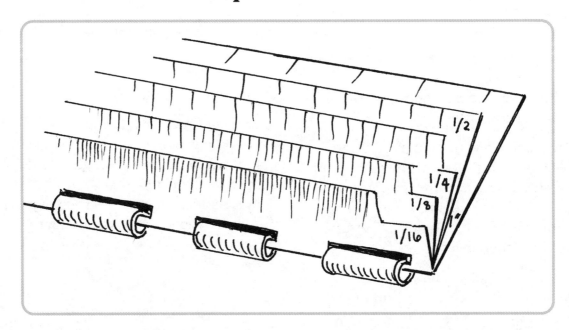

EXPLANATION

The Master Ruler is perfect for students who learn best by measuring one step at a time. It comes in both customary and metric versions.

This ruler works like a flipbook. Large in size, transparent, and very readable, it is five separate rulers in one. Its binding allows students to flip over each unit of measure, starting with one-inch increments, flipping and adding the half-inch increments, and then adding the quarter-inch, eighth-inch, and sixteenth-inch increments, respectively.

The Master Ruler is great for students who are easily confused by all the fractional markings on a customary ruler.

Since the ruler is transparent, you can use it as an overhead teaching tool and demonstrate and interact with small or large groups of students as they learn.

MATERIALS

The Master Ruler is available from:

Crystal Springs Books
75 Jaffrey Rd.
P.O. Box 500
Peterborough, NH 03458
Phone: 1-800-321-0401
Internet: www.crystalsprings.com

A DIFFERENT PATHWAY
Help students learn to understand and measure to the closest unit.

What's My Name?

EXPLANATION

You will need a name tag for each student in the room.

Give each student a name tag with a math fact the class is studying written in the space where the student's name would normally be written. Do not include the answer to the fact on the name tag.

Have students mingle around the room learning the new names of their classmates. For example, Jim's name tag says "3×7" instead of "Jim." Thus, his new name is "21." For the week, everyone must address Jim as "21."

Students can get new names as often as you deem appropriate: daily, twice a week, or weekly.

This activity gets students involved and motivated to learn math facts in a different way.

A DIFFERENT PATHWAY
Reinforce math facts in a new, motivational way.

83

Box One, Circle the Other

EXPLANATION

Avoid the confusion and common mistakes made by students when computing math examples with mixed operations.

On a page of math examples, circle the addition examples and box the subtraction examples.

Have the students do all the addition examples first and correct them. Next, have the students complete all the subtraction examples and correct them.

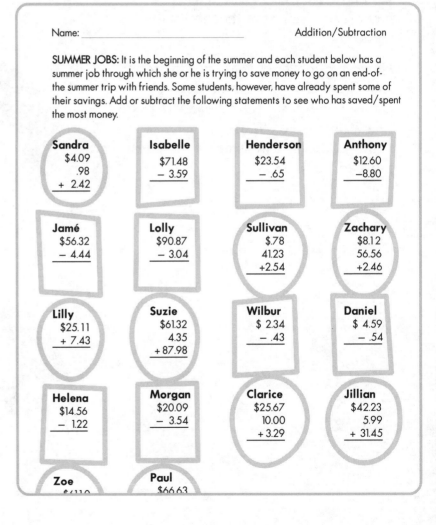

Name: _____   Addition/Subtraction

SUMMER JOBS: It is the beginning of the summer and each student below has a summer job through which she or he is trying to save money to go on an end-of-the summer trip with friends. Some students, however, have already spent some of their savings. Add or subtract the following statements to see who has saved/spent the most money.

Sandra	Isabelle	Henderson	Anthony
$4.09	$71.48	$23.54	$12.60
.98	− 3.59	− .65	−8.80
+ 2.42			

Jamé	Lolly	Sullivan	Zachary
$56.32	$90.87	$.78	$8.12
− 4.44	− 3.04	41.23	56.56
		+2.54	+2.46

Lilly	Suzie	Wilbur	Daniel
$25.11	$61.32	$ 2.34	$ 4.59
+ 7.43	4.35	− .43	− .54
	+ 87.98		

Helena	Morgan	Clarice	Jillian
$14.56	$20.09	$25.67	$42.23
− 1.22	− 3.54	10.00	5.99
		+ 3.29	+ 31.45

Zoe	Paul
$411.0	$66.63

A DIFFERENT PATHWAY
Reduce careless math errors while boosting
a student's confidence.

Keep Your Numbers in Line

EXPLANATION

Prevent careless computation errors made by students with "drifting" handwriting by turning lined paper sideways to facilitate proper number placement. Use graph paper for long division.

See reproducibles in the Appendix on pages 125–128.

GOOD LUCK WITH YOUR ADDITION!

```
  3 4 6      6 3 1      4 4 8
+ 5 5 0    + 7 8 0    + 5 5 1


  8 7 0      3 3 6      4 0 0 8
  9 4 0      4 7 7      2 5 7 3
+ 6 8 8    + 2 3 6    + 7 6 0 1
```

A DIFFERENT PATHWAY
Prevent careless computation errors due to improper number alignment.

Cross Out Every Other Math Example

EXPLANATION

With a light-colored marker, cross out every other math example on a page. Use this as a way to adjust the assignment and create a reasonable workload for discouraged and/or overwhelmed learners.

The examples that are crossed out become either the student's homework assignment or the next day's math lesson.

This curriculum modification is most beneficial to students who work at a much slower pace than others.

Name: _____

CLASS TRIP

The students in the class below are soon leaving for a class trip. Who will bringing the most amount of money on the trip? The least? Solve these prol to find out the answer!

Simone	Gail	Nomar	Jac
$4.09	$5.23	$7.02	$
.98	71.48	23.54	5
+ 6.42	+ 3.59	+ .65	+

Roberto	Sky	Gregory	Mo
$56.32	$90.87	$.78	
4.44	3.04	41.23	
+ 23.87	+ .45	+ 2.54	+

Lucy	Sarah	Washington	Aut
25.11	$61.32	$59.00	$4
+ 7.43	4.35	2.34	
	+ 87.98	+ .43	+

Hector	Monica	Clara
$90.01	$20.09	$25.67
14.56	3.54	10.00
+ 1.22	+ 23.42	+ 3.29

Josephine	Regis	Athlea

A DIFFERENT PATHWAY
Modify the workload for slower-paced students.

Focusing on the Facts

EXPLANATION

Multiplication charts can be too "busy" for many learners. Students can slide multiplication and division facts into focus by using color strips. The high-lighting strips reinforce fact-family relationships.

You will need the master multiplication chart in this book's Appendix. You will also need two different colors of transparency material. (Colored transparency sheets are sold in office-supply stores. A less expensive option is to use colored, transparent book report covers, also available at most office-supply stores.)

Make copies of the reproducible master multiplication chart on page 129 in the Appendix.

Using the master multiplication chart as a pattern, cut out two strips of colored acetate or transparency

material in two different colors. These strips should fit the rows and columns of the master multiplication chart.

Place one colored strip on a column of the chart and place a different-colored strip over a row. For example, try placing one strip, vertically, on the 4's column. Place the other colored strip on the 3's row. You will see the product, 12, come into focus.

Show students how to slide the strips to bring multiplication and division facts into focus.

1	2	3	4	5	6	7	8	9	10	11	12
2	4	6	8	10	12	14	16	18	20	22	24
3	6	9	12	15	18	21	24	27	30	33	36
4	8	12	16	20	24	28	32	36	40	44	48
5	10	15	20	25	30	35	40	45	50	55	60
6	12	18	24	30	36	42	48	54	60	66	72
7	14	21	28	35	42	49	56	63	70	77	84
8	16	24	32	40	48	56	64	72	80	88	96
9	18	27	36	45	54	63	72	81	90	99	108
10	20	30	40	50	60	70	80	90	100	110	120
11	22	33	44	55	66	77	88	99	110	121	132
12	24	36	48	60	72	84	96	108	120	132	144

A DIFFERENT PATHWAY
Use a multiplication chart to reinforce
number-family relationships.

Equivalent Fractions Before Your Eyes

EXPLANATION

A multiplication chart is a great tool for showing number patterns and relationships, and it's ideal for students to use for finding equivalent fractions.

To assemble a chart, use the reproducible on page 129 in the Appendix and some colored acetate strips.

To begin, place one acetate strip horizontally on the first row of numbers on the multiplication chart. Next, place the second strip directly below it.

As you look at the two rows covered by the colored strips, think "fractions" instead of two rows of numbers. You should see the equivalent fractions for 1/2: 2/4, 4/8, 6/12, and so on.

Next, place the strips across the rows beginning with 2 and 3. Now the equivalent fractions for 2/3 become clear.

By moving the colored strips down the rows, equivalent fractions through 11/12 are shown on the chart.

Students can also place the colored strips on nonadjacent rows to find the equivalent fractions for examples such as 3/8, 2/7, 5/9, 6/10, and so on.

1	2	3	4	5	6	7	8	9	10	11	12
2	4	6	8	10	12	14	16	18	20	22	24
3	6	9	12	15	18	21	24	27	30	33	36
4	8	12	16	20	24	28	32	36	40	44	48
5	10	15	20	25	30	35	40	45	50	55	60
6	12	18	24	30	36	42	48	54	60	66	72
7	14	21	28	35	42	49	56	63	70	77	84
8	16	24	32	40	48	56	64	72	80	88	96
9	18	27	36	45	54	63	72	81	90	99	108
10	20	30	40	50	60	70	80	90	100	110	120
11	22	33	44	55	66	77	88	99	110	121	132
12	24	36	48	60	72	84	96	108	120	132	144

A DIFFERENT PATHWAY
Use a multiplication chart to find and reinforce equivalent fractions.

Not Your Average Math Practice

EXPLANATION

This is a great method to introduce and practice finding the average of a set of numbers.

You will need a hundreds chart (see reproducible in the Appendix on page 130), transparent counters (magnetic bingo chips work well), and a calculator to check your computations.

Make an overhead transparency of the hundreds chart to demonstrate and work on this activity with the class using the overhead projector.

Start by finding the squares on the chart with the numbers 1, 3, 21, and 23. (See the illustration.) Place bingo chips of the same color on all of these squares.

Have the class find the sum of these four numbers (48).

Then ask the students to divide the sum by the number of squares they added (48 ÷ 4 = 12). Use a different-colored bingo chip to cover the square with the number 12.

Have students describe the pattern they see with this type of averaging; then ask them to choose four new numbers and predict the average.

Note: This activity also works on calendars and multiplication charts. The key is to find a square on the chart with an *odd number* of sides. The average number is always the center number in the square.

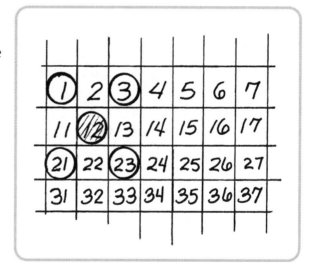

A DIFFERENT PATHWAY
Find averages by using manipulatives and hundreds charts.

89

Howdy, Partner Factor!

EXPLANATION

This method teaches students how to factor numbers in a way that reinforces multiplication/division relationships.

Refer to the illustration for a visual cue on this method.

To begin, students draw a vertical line on their paper.

They then write the "target number" (i.e., the number they are factoring) in the upper right corner, to the right of the line.

Next, they write the number 1 opposite the target number, to the left of the vertical line. (The number 1 is a factor of every number.)

They then begin the questioning: "Is 2 a factor?" If 2 is a factor of the number, they write a 2 below the 1, to the left of the vertical line. Then they put its "partner" directly opposite it, to the right of the vertical line.

They continue with 3, 4, 5, and so on, until they have listed all the factors of the target number.

A DIFFERENT PATHWAY
Factor numbers and reinforce number-family relationships.

What's Your Response?

EXPLANATION

The use of response cards is a management technique that helps you assess the understanding of individual students within a large-group setting.

Give each student three white index cards.

They write YES on the first card, NO on the second, and a question mark on the third.

Students can store their response cards in library-book pockets kept inside their desks or binders.

Instruct students that no one is allowed to look at anyone else's response card, nor is anyone to ask another student how he/she responded. When asked a question, students should choose the appropriate response card and then hold it up just below their chin for the teacher to check their understanding.

Tell students you will ask them to take out their response cards periodically throughout the day to respond to instructions or directions. For example, you might read aloud and stop to ask the class to predict if they think a particular event will happen in the story. In math class, you might write a number on the board and ask the class to respond about whether they agree that it is an even number. You might also give multi-step directions before a lesson and ask the students to use their response cards to show whether they understand.

This technique helps students learn to focus and pay attention.

A DIFFERENT PATHWAY
Assess individual understanding in a large-group setting.

91

Anecdotal Records

EXPLANATION

Patterns of information help teachers make decisions about interventions that work with students. Anecdotal records are an effective way to keep track of your observations during "kid-watching" time.

Photocopy a blank monthly calendar (see reproducible in the Appendix on page 131) for each student in your class.

When you want to record an observation about a student, take out that student's monthly calendar and write the following:

- Next to B, write the behavior you are watching.
- Next to I, write the intervention you are trying.
- Next to R, write the result of the intervention.

This type of record shows patterns of behaviors, what intervention you have already used in an effort to help, and the result of the efforts. This information is helpful for making instructional decisions for students.

THE MONTHLY MANAGER

Month of _September_   Student's Name _Robin Jenkins_

	Monday	Tuesday	Wednesday	Thursday	Friday
Week of 9/23 to 9/27	**B:** Writes "My brother don't" in his narrative. **I:** Demonstrated how to whisper read into the Phonics Phone to catch usage concern. **R:** Corrected 3 out of 4 usage concerns.	**B:** **I:** **R:**	**B:** **I:** **R:**	**B:** **I:** **R:**	**B:** **I:** **R:**
Week of to	**B:** **I:** **R:**	**B:** **I:** **R:**	**B:** **I:** **R:**	**B:** **I:** **R:**	**B:** **I:** **R:**
Week of to	**B:** **I:** **R:**	**B:** **I:** **R:**	**B:** **I:** **R:**	**B:** **I:** **R:**	**B:** **I:** **R:**
Week of to	**B:** **I:** **R:**	**B:** **I:** **R:**	**B:** **I:** **R:**	**B:** **I:** **R:**	**B:** **I:** **R:**
Week of to	**B:** **I:** **R:**	**B:** **I:** **R:**	**B:** **I:** **R:**	**B:** **I:** **R:**	**B:** **I:** **R:**

B= Behavior   I= Intervention   R= Result

A DIFFERENT PATHWAY
Gather important anecdotal information about students and their learning.

Level the Playing Field

EXPLANATION

Separate language from computation by using a copier to eliminate word problems from math papers with basic math examples.

Non-readers and ELL (English Language Learners) students will be able to experi-ence math-computation success with this simple curriculum modification.

Word problems can be presented in due time when the student becomes a better reader and/or English proficient.

Name: _____   Addition/Subtraction

Write out and solve these story problems.

EXAMPLE
1. Rob had $.98. He spent $.50 for a candy bar. How much money does Rob have left?

$.98
.50
$.48

2. Timmy had 23 pennies. He gave 11 pennies to his sister. How many pen-nies does Timmy have left?
_____ pennies

3. Walker bought a piece of pizza for $1.00 and a soda for $.59. How much did Walker spend in all?
$_____

4. Rob and Timmy hiked 12 miles the first day and 9 miles the second day. How many miles did they hike both days?
_____ miles.

Add or subtract

| 21 | 56 | 47 |
| +12 | − 33 | + 22 |

| 23 | 36 | 10 |
| −19 | + 27 | − 6 |

Add or subtract

| 21 | 56 | 47 |
| +12 | − 33 | + 22 |

| 23 | 36 | 10 |
| −19 | + 27 | − 6 |

A DIFFERENT PATHWAY

Use an equitable method to assess math proficiency in a way that separates language from computation.

93

One, Two, Three…Go!

EXPLANATION

This process helps teachers ensure a student is correctly doing a math process or writing spelling words before doing several examples on his/her own. Practice makes permanent, so you want to be sure that what the student is practicing is correct.

When learning new algorithms in math or writing new spelling words, some students get off to an incorrect start and reinforce it by completing several examples, if not an entire page, before a teacher catches the problem.

To prevent this, use the One, Two, Three…Go! method of monitoring student work. A student does one example and then checks with you or a pre-assigned student. If the example is correct, the student then does two examples in a row and returns for feedback. If those examples are done accurately, the student completes three in a row and checks in. If those are correct, tell the student it's a go! He/she can complete the assignment, reinforcing that practice makes permanent.

A DIFFERENT PATHWAY
Monitor and ensure a student's understanding before "practice makes permanent."

Personal-Learning Time Lines

EXPLANATION

This is a unique strategy for journaling. Use rolls of fax paper or adding-machine tape for students to unroll at the end of each day to capture the day's important learning.

Each student needs his/her own personal roll of paper. You can store them all together in one safe box, or students can keep them in their desks or cubbies.

During the last 20 minutes of the school day, have a reflect-and-regroup time. Students take out their learning time lines and unroll them to the next free space.

Here they write the date on the space and then record or draw important highlights of the day's learning.

Students can write examples of math problems they worked on, new vocabulary words learned, titles of completed books, illustrations of special events, poems they have written, and so forth.

The time lines help students see their own learning in progress, and they also serve as excellent records for parents to keep at the end of the school year.

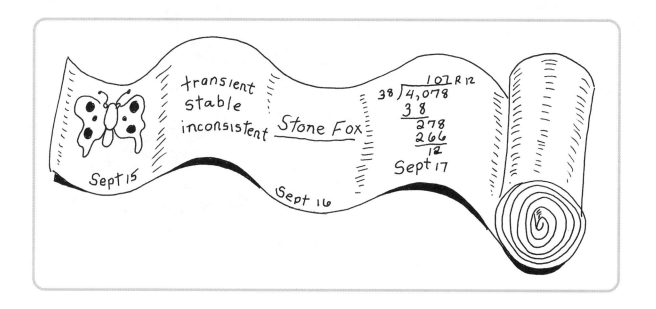

A DIFFERENT PATHWAY
Help students keep an ongoing record and time line
of their daily learning.

95

High-Tech Assessment

EXPLANATION

At the beginning of the school year, start a personal videotape for each student, as well as one for the entire class. It's an excellent way to capture the learning and the memories. Videotaping also provides immediate visual and auditory feedback for students to assess and improve their learning.

Throughout the year, record individual successes and important group events on the videotape.

Weave in state-standard requirements, as well as curriculum goals for language arts, as students give presentations on videotape.

Allow some students to submit videotapes as projects to show what they have learned.

A DIFFERENT PATHWAY
Capture student events and work samples throughout the school year.

Student-Led Conferences

EXPLANATION

A student-led conference involves the student, parent(s), and teacher(s). It creates a critical partnership with the parent(s) or guardian(s) and draws them into their child's education beyond the typical "bake sale" involvement.

Professional books on the topic of student-led conferences are available, but basically such a conference is a situation where both the student and parent(s) attend.

During the conference, the student reviews and explains his/her portfolio or work samples from the marking period. You discuss the grading system, and together you, the student, and the parent(s) establish goals to help with study or academic skills. At the next conference, the first order of business is to review progress toward these goals.

A DIFFERENT PATHWAY
Create a student/teacher/parent partnership and review and assess the learning process and progress.

Here's Looking at You, Kid

EXPLANATION

Report cards should demonstrate a student's growth in all areas of instruction for the marking period. The problem with many graded report cards is the difficulty of attaching a letter grade to student performance. Anecdotal reports can be time consuming, and sometimes parents do not take the time to read them. An alternative kind of report card (see reproducible on page 132 in the Appendix) is a one-page summary of the marking period's focus of instruction and a record of the student's progress.

It is a straightforward form.

This report card is also responsive to the needs of special-education students who have modified curriculums and for whom a traditional report card is not appropriate.

A DIFFERENT PATHWAY
Report actual student progress without giving letter grades.

Facts in a Flash

EXPLANATION

This game is a great activity for reviewing, practicing, and assessing students' learning of a particular skill or unit of study.

You will need one index card for each student in your class.

To begin, create a T chart. At the top of the left column, write the phrase "I Have," and at the top of the right column, write the phrase "Who Has?"

Choose a skill or unit of study for review. For example, to review math facts, you might create a T chart like this:

I Have	Who Has?
25	The square root of my number?
5	This number, plus 14 more?
19	This number, take away 7?
12	This number doubled?
24	This number, plus 6, minus 5?
25	

The number or fact that is your beginning point should also be your end point. Each card has an entire row recorded on it, such as "I have 25; who has the square root of my number?"

When playing this game, the class sits in a circle. One student starts the fast-fact session. When his/her answer comes up again, the game is over. Try beating a timer!

A DIFFERENT PATHWAY
Help students practice or review what they have been studying.

Realistic Rubrics

Fluent Facts!	Accurate, Not Fluent	Emergent Learning Stage
30 facts/min. paper & pencil	15 facts/min. paper & pencil	>10 facts/min. paper & pencil
40 facts/min. oral	20 facts/min. oral	>15 facts/min. oral
Knows facts at a level of automaticity.	Automatic knowledge of math facts in instructional situations is inconsistent.	Needs intervention or assistance most of the time.

EXPLANATION

Rubrics function as diagnostic, prescriptive, and evaluative tools. They help us assess individual, as well as small and large group instructional needs. Rubrics allow us to focus on interventions, methods, or strategies that are appropriate for students. They also provide the criteria through which student performance will be evaluated for specific projects, assignments, or units of study.

You can create your own rubrics for most aspects of your classroom program. Just follow these simple steps:

Decide on the purpose of your rubric. For example, you might want to assess, plan, and/or monitor the progress of your students' math fact fluency.

Next, determine the mastery levels and use these as labels for each column on your grid. Then, add indicators below each mastery label that describe representative performance levels.

A DIFFERENT PATHWAY
Assess, plan, and monitor instruction and learning.

Dueling Charts

EXPLANATION

Select a topic that your students have been studying, such as the Civil War.

Write the topic phrase (in this case, "Civil War") horizontally across each of two charts.

Divide students into two teams.

Each team lines up behind one chart.

On a given signal, a student from each team goes to the chart and writes a phrase pertaining to something studied from the unit. The first phrase must start with the first letter of the phrase you have written on the chart. For example, "Civil War began in 1861." The next student from each team writes a phrase that starts with the second letter of the phrase you have written on the chart, and so on.

The first team to finish gets a high-five from the other team.

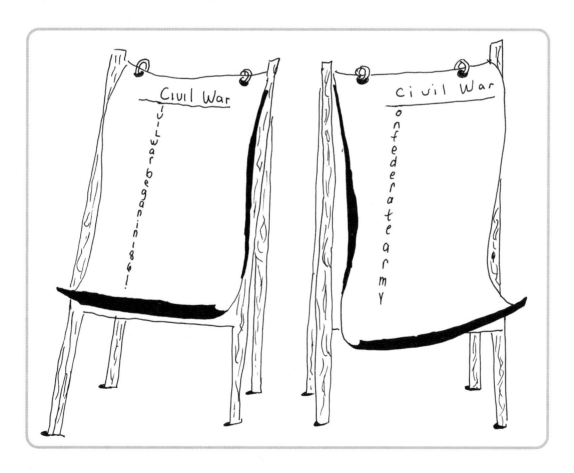

Appendix

Student Problem Report

Filed by: _____

Date: _____

Description of Problem: _____

_____

_____

Location of Problem: _____

_____

Persons Involved: _____

_____

Witnesses: _____

_____

What did the witnesses do? _____

_____

How do you feel about what happened? _____

_____

How do you think the other student feels? _____

_____

List two things you might have done to solve the problem or prevent it from happening:

1. _____

2. _____

What do you think the teacher should do about this problem?

_____

_____

Student signature _____

I'd Mark with the Sunshine

by Kalli Dakos

If I were a teacher,
I wouldn't mark in red,
Because red reminds me
Of blood that
Oozes out of cuts,
And fire engines that
Rush to fight blazes
So hot you could
Die in them,
And STOP signs that
Warn you of danger.

If I were a teacher
I'd mark in yellow—
For corn muffins,
Mustard on a fat hot dog,
Gardens of dandelions,
And sunbeams that
Dance on daffodils.

If I were a teacher,
I'd throw out my STOP pen,
And I'd mark with
The sunshine itself!
To give light to an *A*,
Warmth to a *C*,
And hope to an *F*.

Left-Hander Factoids

- There are twice as many left-handed boys as girls.

- Left-handers are twice as likely to qualify for membership in Mensa, the high-IQ society.

- One person in ten is left-handed.

- One-third of all presidents since 1945 has been left-handed.

- President Ronald Reagan was born left-handed, then switched.

- Left-handed people tend to have more industrial accidents.

- Left-handed people have a more acute sense of humor. Left-handed comics include:
  W.C. Fields, Harpo Marx, Carol Burnett, David Letterman, Charlie Chaplin, Richard Pryor, Jay Leno, and Dick VanDyke.

- The French horn is valved for the left hand.

- Michelangelo was left-handed.

- Almost one-half of the major league batting and pitching stars are left-handed.

- Toll booths favor left-handers.

- Ben Franklin was left-handed.

- Hand preference is evident by age five.

- Joan of Arc was left-handed.

- Billy the Kid was left-handed.

Adapted from: *Left-Handed Kids: Why Are They So Different?* and *The Natural Superiority of the Left-Hander* by James T. DeKay, and *Left-Handed in a Right-Handed World* by Jeff Goldsmith.

10 Homework Tips for Parents

1. Set aside a specific time for your child to do homework each night. This will help eliminate procrastination.

2. Designate a quiet and well-lit place for your child to work.

3. Protect your child from annoying distractions. Establish a quiet zone.

4. Be sure your child has the necessary materials and supplies at hand to support his/her homework (e.g., pencil, pen, eraser, pencil sharpener, ruler, paper, etc.). Create a "school-office" atmosphere for your child.

5. Stay in close proximity to your child during homework time.

6. Have your child invite a study buddy over to do homework together.

7. If you are unable to help your child with an assignment, find a relative, neighbor, or older student who is willing to help out.

8. Always check your child's homework for quality and completeness.

9. Connect with your child's school on a regular basis. Know the school's homework policy, ask how you can support what the school is doing, and question the amount of homework and the purpose of the assignments. Inquire if daily and long-term homework assignments are posted on the school's web site.

10. Homework should be thought of as an extension of your child's classroom. It is an opportunity for your child to review, practice, and rehearse material that has been previously taught.

Individual Adaptation Plan – Form A

Student: _____ **Date:** _____

Curriculum Modifications

Goal: _____

_____

Modifications: _____

_____

_____

_____

_____

_____

Implemented by: _____

Title/Role: _____

Progress Review

Date: _____

Comments: _____

_____

_____

_____

_____

_____

_____

_____

Goal: _____

_____

Modifications: _____

_____

_____

_____

_____

_____

Implemented by: _____

Title/Role: _____

Progress Review

Date: _____

Comments: _____

_____

_____

_____

_____

_____

_____

_____

Goal: _____

_____

Modifications: _____

_____

_____

_____

_____

_____

Implemented by: _____

Title/Role: _____

Progress Review

Date: _____

Comments: _____

_____

_____

_____

_____

_____

_____

_____

Individual Adaptation Plan – Form B

Student: _____ Date: _____

Instructional Accommodations

Goal: _____

_____

Accommodations: _____

_____

_____

_____

_____

_____

Implemented by: _____

Title/Role: _____

Progress Review

Date: _____

Comments: _____

_____

_____

_____

_____

_____

_____

_____

Goal: _____

_____

Accommodations: _____

_____

_____

_____

_____

_____

_____

Implemented by: _____

Title/Role: _____

Progress Review

Date: _____

Comments: _____

_____

_____

_____

_____

_____

_____

_____

Goal: _____

_____

Accommodations: _____

_____

_____

_____

_____

_____

Implemented by: _____

Title/Role: _____

Progress Review

Date: _____

Comments: _____

_____

_____

_____

_____

_____

_____

_____

Individual Adaptation Plan – Form C

Student: _____ Date: _____

Additional Intervention Programs and Services

Goal:_____ _____ Intervention/Programs/Services:_____ _____ _____ _____ _____ _____ _____ Implemented by: _____ Title/Role: _____	**Progress Review** Date: _____ Comments: _____ _____ _____ _____ _____ _____ _____ _____
Goal:_____ _____ Intervention/Programs/Services:_____ _____ _____ _____ _____ _____ _____ Implemented by: _____ Title/Role: _____	**Progress Review** Date: _____ Comments: _____ _____ _____ _____ _____ _____ _____ _____
Goal:_____ _____ Intervention/Programs/Services:_____ _____ _____ _____ _____ _____ _____ Implemented by: _____ Title/Role: _____	**Progress Review** Date: _____ Comments: _____ _____ _____ _____ _____ _____ _____ _____

No Can'ts Allowed

I can do

_____

Name _____

Date _____

I can do

_____

Name _____

Date _____

I can do

_____

Name _____

Date _____

I can do

_____

Name _____

Date _____

Differentiated Instruction. © Crystal Springs Books. Permission for the reproduction of this page is limited to the local school site that has purchased this book.

Clock Partners

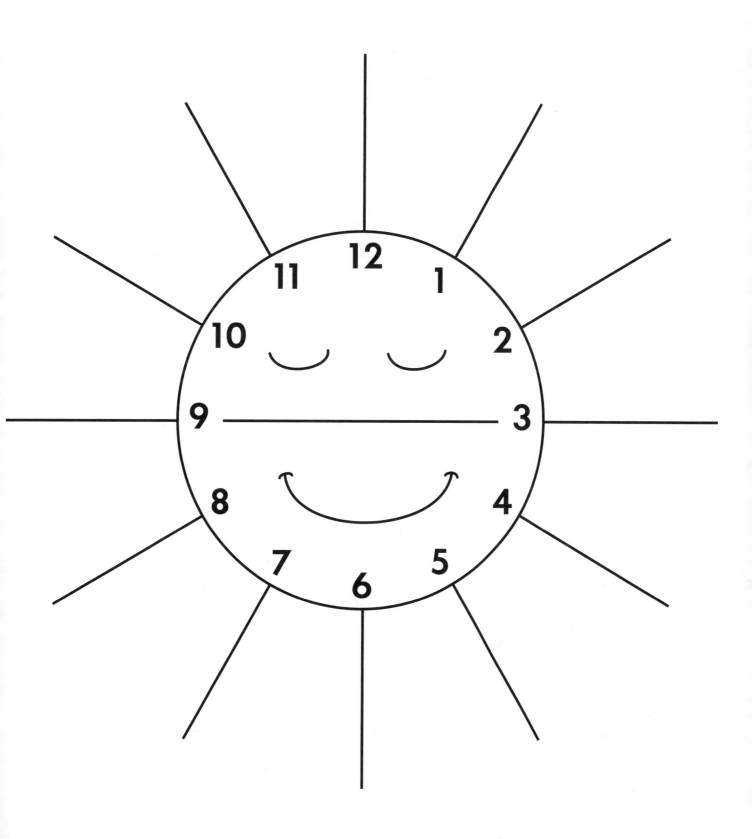

Multiple Intelligence Scavenger Hunt

Find someone who:

Reads every night

_____

Keeps a journal

_____

Makes quilts

_____

Fixes engines

_____

Sings in a chorus

_____

Can whistle our national anthem

_____

Can finish this sequence: 1, 1, 2, 3, 5, 8 . . .

_____

Can define *icosahedron*

_____

Will recite a short poem

_____

Plays a sport

_____

Takes dance lessons

_____

Plays an instrument

_____

Loves to entertain

_____

Can juggle

_____

Makes art

_____

Enjoys hiking or camping

_____

Likes to take things apart

_____

BUZZ SHEET

DISCUSS THE QUESTIONS WITH YOUR PARTNER

GETTING STARTED

1. WHAT IS YOUR FAVORITE . . . WHY?
   * PLACE TO GO ON VACATION
   * WAY TO TRAVEL
   * PLACE TO EAT
   * PLACE TO SPEND THE NIGHT

FEELING COMFORTABLE

2. WHEN WAS THE LAST TIME YOU FELT ONE OF THESE . . . WHY?

   * HAPPY   * PUT DOWN
   * COOL   * EMBARRASSED
   * ZANY   * EXCITED

CURRENT FEELINGS

3. WHICH THREE MENU ITEMS BEST DESCRIBE YOUR FEELINGS NOW? WHY?

   * HAMBURGER   * MILKSHAKE
   * CHERRY COKE   * PIZZA
   * OREO COOKIES   * JELLO

Numbers Chart

1	2	3	4	5	6	7	8	9	10
2	4	6	8	10	12	14	16	18	20
3	6	9	12	15	18	21	24	27	30
4	8	12	16	20	24	28	32	36	40
5	10	15	20	25	30	35	40	45	50
6	12	18	24	30	36	42	48	54	60
7	14	21	28	35	42	49	56	63	70
8	16	24	32	40	48	56	64	72	80
9	18	27	36	45	54	63	72	81	90
10	20	30	40	50	60	70	80	90	100

Focus Frame

DIRECTIONS:

Cut out and trace Focus Frame pattern below onto poster board or equivalent stock paper. Cut out focus frame from poster board, then cut along lines (indicated on pattern) on frame section A. Insert frame section B into section A to form a movable box. Slide the Focus Frame to adjust for the amount of space needed.

Student slides Focus Frame to fit the present problem.

Eliminates unnecessary information or distractions. ➔

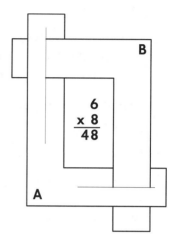

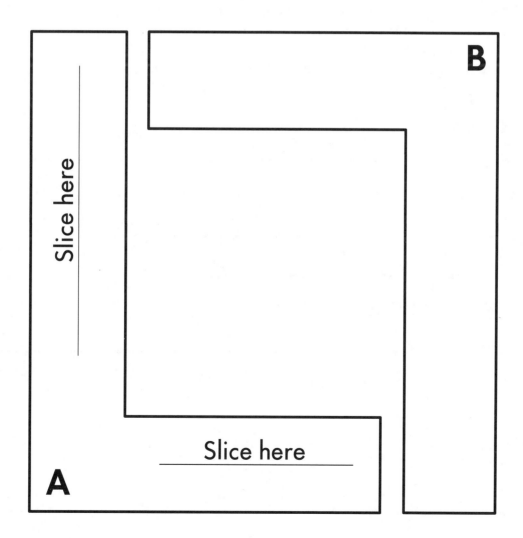

Sliding Mask

DIRECTIONS:

- Cut Mask (A) and Strip (B) pattern out and trace onto poster board or equivalent stock paper.

- Cut along inside line and remove paper to reveal open window.

- Place open window over desired text/problems, then slide paper/plastic strip (from underneath the Mask) to cover or reveal selected text/problems.

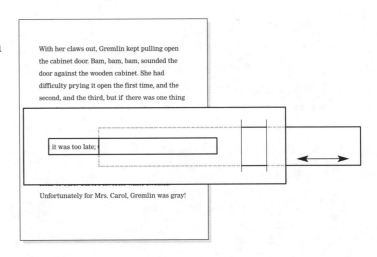

With her claws out, Gremlin kept pulling open the cabinet door. Bam, bam, bam, sounded the door against the wooden cabinet. She had difficulty prying it open the first time, and the second, and the third, but if there was one thing

it was too late;

Unfortunately for Mrs. Carol, Gremlin was gray!

Note: The Sliding Mask can be modified by taping a colored plastic strip (colored acetate or frosted colored overlays, for example) over the window opening. This is particularly helpful for students who experience difficulty when reading black print on white paper. See page 56 for more information on colored overlays.

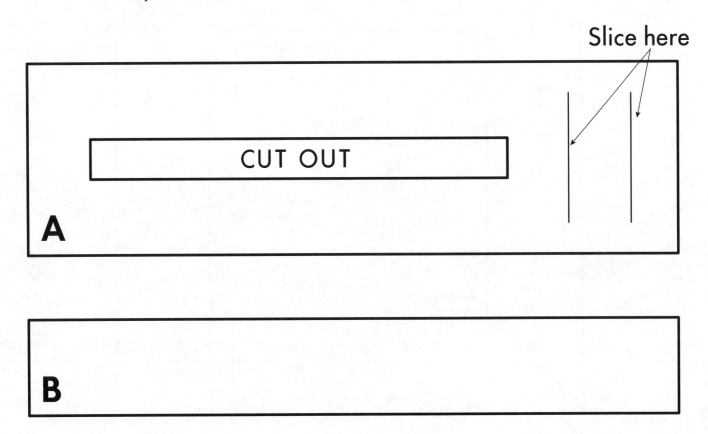

Slice here

CUT OUT

A

B

Self-Test

Do you or someone you know have difficulty reading?
Take the following test:

	YES	NO
Do you skip words or lines when reading?		
Do you reread lines?		
Do you lose your place?		
Are you easily distracted when reading?		
Do you need to take breaks often?		
Do you find it harder to read the longer you read?		
Do you get headaches when you read?		
Do your eyes get red and watery?		
Does reading make you tired?		
Do you blink or squint?		
Do you prefer to read in dim light?		
Do you read close to the page?		
Do you use your finger or other markers?		
Do you get restless, active, or fidgety when reading?		

*If you answered *yes* to three or more of these questions, then you might be experiencing the effects of a perception problem called Scotopic Sensitivity Syndrome.

Adapted with permission from *Reading by the Colors* by Helen L. Irlen, Penguin Putnam/Perigee Div. Publishers.

4-6-8

EVENTS	SETTINGS	CHARACTERS
1.	1.	1.
2.	2.	
3.	3.	2.
4.	4.	
5.	5.	3.
6.	6.	
7.		4.
8.		

Differentiated Instruction.

WORD MAP

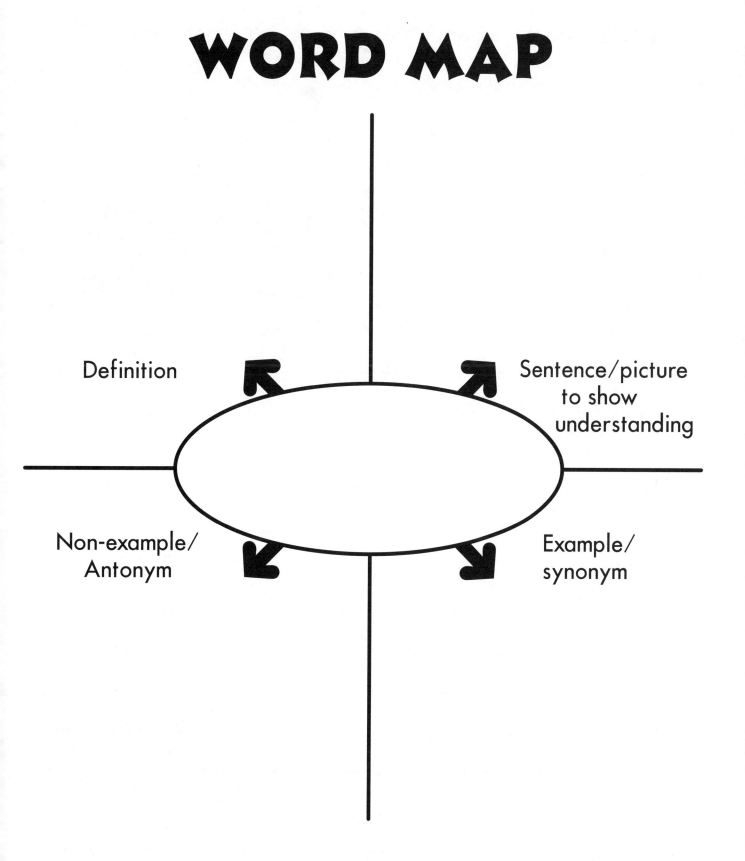

Definition

Sentence/picture to show understanding

Non-example/ Antonym

Example/ synonym

C.P.S.R. Response Starters

What did you think about the sentences your partner picked?

○ *I liked this part because* _____

_____

○ *I didn't like this part because* _____

_____

○ *This scene made me think about* _____

_____

○ *I wonder* _____

_____

○ *I didn't understand why* _____

_____

○ *I can't believe* _____

_____

○ *I think* _____

_____

○ *I feel* _____

_____

○ *I wish* _____ *had happened.*

_____

○ *If I were (character's name), I* _____

_____

FOOD ALLERGY ACTION PLAN

ALLERGY TO: _____

Student's
Name: _____ D.O.B.: _____ Teacher: _____

Asthmatic: ❏ Yes, high risk for severe reaction ❏ No

Place Child's
Picture Here

SIGNS OF AN ALLERGIC REACTION

SYSTEMS   **SYMPTOMS**

- **MOUTH**   itching and swelling of the lips, tongue, or mouth
- **THROAT***   itching and/or a sense of tightness in the throat, hoarseness, and hacking cough
- **SKIN**   hives, itchy rash, and/or swelling about the face or extremities
- **GUT**   nausea, abdominal cramps, vomiting, and/or diarrhea
- **LUNG***   shortness of breath, repetitive coughing, and/or wheezing
- **HEART***   "thready" pulse, "passing out"

The severity of symptoms can quickly change.
* All above symptoms can potentially progress to a life-threatening situation.

ACTION FOR MINOR REACTION

1. If only symptom(s) are: _____, give _____
                                                                   (MEDICATION/DOSE/ROUTE)

_____

Then call:

2. Mother: _____, Father: _____, or emergency contacts.

3. Dr. _____ at _____.

If condition does not improve within 10 minutes, follow steps for Major Reaction, below.

ACTION FOR MAJOR REACTION

1. If ingestion is suspected and/or symptom(s) are:_____

give _____ IMMEDIATELY!
                               (MEDICATION/DOSE/ROUTE)

Then call:

2. Rescue Squad (ask for advanced life support)

3. Mother: _____, Father: _____, or emergency contacts.

4. Dr. _____ at _____.

DO NOT HESITATE TO CALL RESCUE SQUAD!

Parent's   Doctor's
Signature: _____ Date: _____ Signature: _____ Date: _____

Food Allergy Action Plan, *continued*

EMERGENCY CONTACTS	**TRAINED STAFF MEMBERS**
1. _____	**1.** _____
Relation: _____ Phone: _____	Room: _____
2. _____	**2.** _____
Relation: _____ Phone: _____	Room: _____
3. _____	**3.** _____
Relation: _____ Phone: _____	Room: _____

EPIPEN ® AND EPIPEN ® JR. DIRECTIONS

1. Pull off gray safety cap.

2. Place black tip on outer thigh (always apply to thigh).

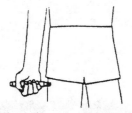

3. Using a quick motion, press hard into thigh until Auto-Injector mechanism functions. Hold in place and count to 10. The EpiPen ® unit should then be removed and discarded. Massage the injection area for 10 seconds.

For children with multiple food allergies, use one form for each food.

To learn more about the Food Allergy and Anaphylaxis Network, go to: www.foodallergy.org.

Adapted with permission from The Food Allergy and Anaphylaxis Network.

Good Luck with Your Addition!

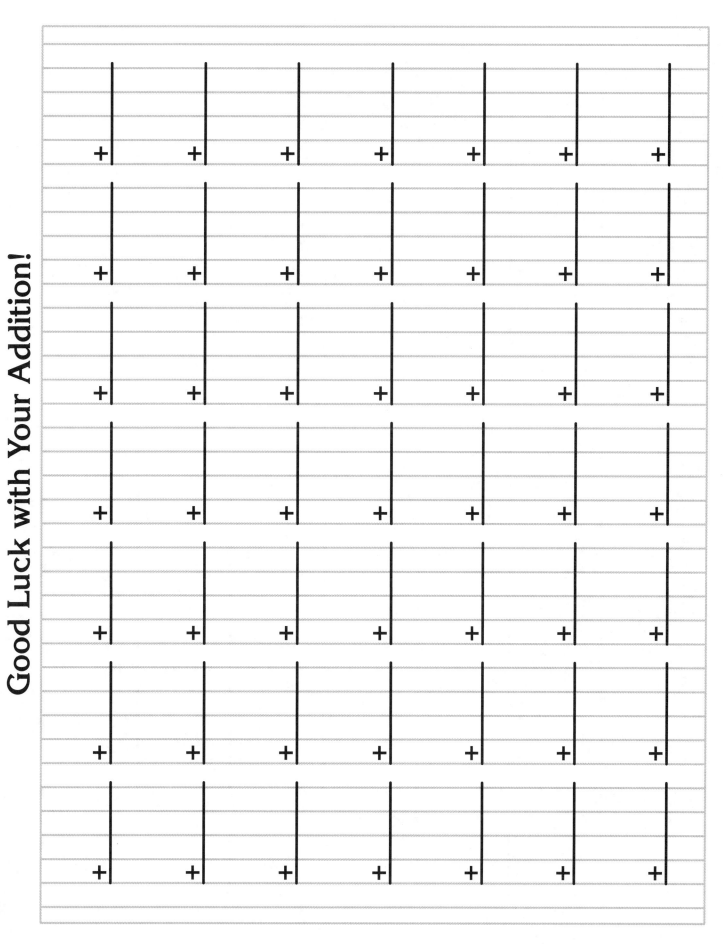

Good Luck with Your Subtraction!

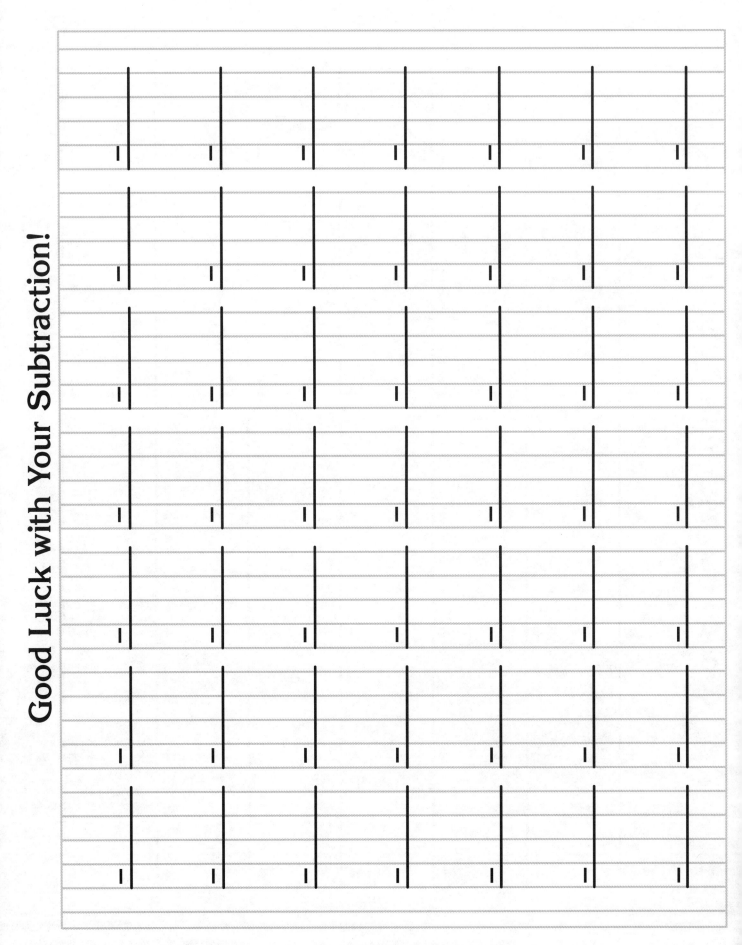

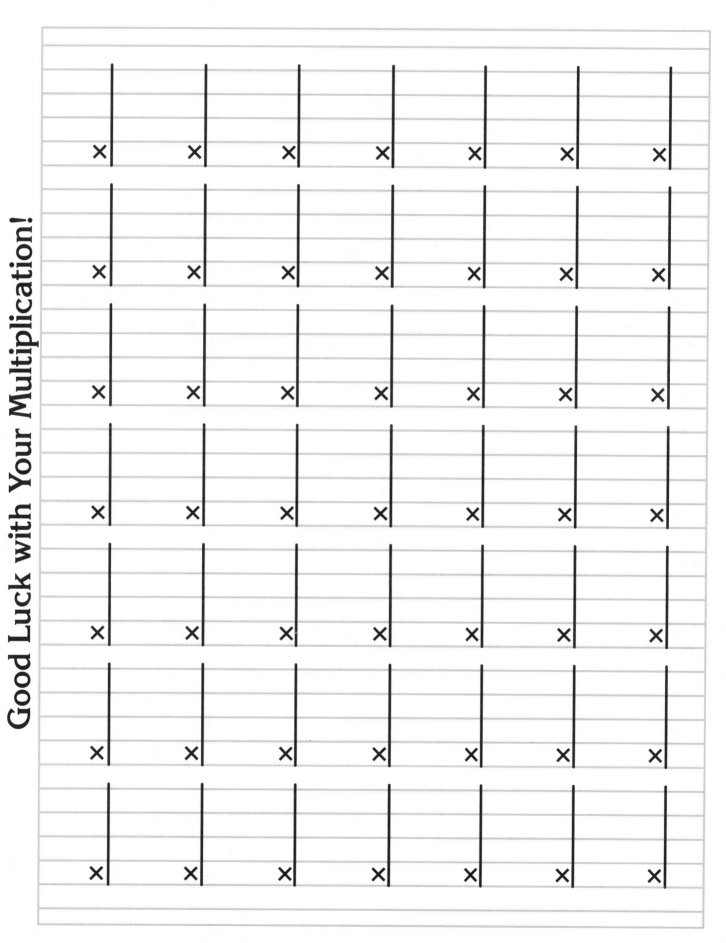

Good Luck with Your Multiplication!

Differentiated Instruction. © Crystal Springs Books. Permission for the reproduction of this page is limited to the local school site that has purchased this book. **127**

Good Luck with Your Division!

Divide ÷   Multiply ✕   **Does McDonald's Sell Cheeseburgers Rare?**
Subtract –   Check ✓   **Bring down**   **Remainder**

Multiplication Chart

DIRECTIONS for Focusing on the Facts:

1. Locate two sheets of colored acetate.

2. Cut out two different colored strips ($\frac{1}{2}" \times 7\frac{1}{2}"$).

3. Choose a "fact family," such as $4 \times 7 = 28$, on the multiplication chart. Lay one colored strip along the 4s row. Lay the other down on the 7s column.

4. The product (or dividend) appears at the intersection of the two strips.

DIRECTIONS for Equivalent Fractions Before Your Eyes:

1. Locate two sheets of colored acetate.

2. Cut out two different colored strips ($\frac{1}{2}" \times 7\frac{1}{2}"$).

3. Find equivalent fractions by placing one strip across one row of numbers and a second strip across another row of numbers.

1	2	3	4	5	6	7	8	9	10	11	12
2	4	6	8	10	12	14	16	18	20	22	24
3	6	9	12	15	18	21	24	27	30	33	36
4	8	12	16	20	24	28	32	36	40	44	48
5	10	15	20	25	30	35	40	45	50	55	60
6	12	18	24	30	36	42	48	54	60	66	72
7	14	21	28	35	42	49	56	63	70	77	84
8	16	24	32	40	48	56	64	72	80	88	96
9	18	27	36	45	54	63	72	81	90	99	108
10	20	30	40	50	60	70	80	90	100	110	120
11	22	33	44	55	66	77	88	99	110	121	132
12	24	36	48	60	72	84	96	108	120	132	144

Hundreds Chart

1	2	3	4	5	6	7	8	9	10
11	12	13	14	15	16	17	18	19	20
21	22	23	24	25	26	27	28	29	30
31	32	33	34	35	36	37	38	39	40
41	42	43	44	45	46	47	48	49	50
51	52	53	54	55	56	57	58	59	60
61	62	63	64	65	66	67	68	69	70
71	72	73	74	75	76	77	78	79	80
81	82	83	84	85	86	87	88	89	90
91	92	93	94	95	96	97	98	99	100

THE MONTHLY MANAGER

Month of _____   Student's Name _____

	Monday	Tuesday	Wednesday	Thursday	Friday
Week of ___ to ___	B: I: R:	B: I: R:	B: I: R:	B: I: R:	B: I: R:
Week of ___ to ___	B: I: R:	B: I: R:	B: I: R:	B: I: R:	B: I: R:
Week of ___ to ___	B: I: R:	B: I: R:	B: I: R:	B: I: R:	B: I: R:
Week of ___ to ___	B: I: R:	B: I: R:	B: I: R:	B: I: R:	B: I: R:
Week of ___ to ___	B: I: R:	B: I: R:	B: I: R:	B: I: R:	B: I: R:

B= Behavior   I= Intervention   R= Result

REPORT CARD

Student Name: _____

Teacher: _____

Grade: _____

Report Period: _____

Spelling

Level: _____

Program: _____

Progress:	C	P	N	/
Effort:	C	P	N	/

Comments:_____

_____

Listening

Follows Directions:	C	P	N	/
Shows Understanding:	C	P	N	/
Enjoys Stories:	C	P	N	/

Comments:_____

_____

Speaking

Expresses Self Clearly:	C	P	N	/
Uses Good Diction:	C	P	N	/
Joins Discussions:	C	P	N	/

Comments:_____

_____

Writing

Writes Interesting Leads:	C	P	N	/
Sequences Ideas:	C	P	N	/
Develops Theme:	C	P	N	/
Uses "Voice" in Story:	C	P	N	/
Uses Grammatical Rules:	C	P	N	/
Uses Legible Penmanship:	C	P	N	/
Writes Strong Endings:	C	P	N	/

Comments:_____

_____

Social/Emotional Growth

Is Cooperative:	C	P	N	/
Accepts Responsibility:	C	P	N	/
Accepts Rules and Limits	C	P	N	/
Uses Self-Control	C	P	N	/

Comments:_____

_____

Reading

Level: _____

Program: _____

Selects Books at Level:	C	P	N	/
Reads Independently:	C	P	N	/
Reads for Meaning:	C	P	N	/
Self-Corrects:	C	P	N	/
Shows Understanding:	C	P	N	/
Sustains Silent Reading:	C	P	N	/
Enjoys Reading:	C	P	N	/
Reads Different Genres	C	P	N	/

Comments:_____

_____

Math Concepts: _____

Approximate Level: _____

Number Facts:	C	P	N	/
Number Sense:	C	P	N	/
Addition:	C	P	N	/
Subtraction:	C	P	N	/
Multiplication:	C	P	N	/
Division:	C	P	N	/
Geometry:	C	P	N	/
Measurement:	C	P	N	/
Problem Solving:	C	P	N	/

Comments:_____

_____

Social Studies/Science

Themes: _____

Participates:	C	P	N	/
Understands Concepts:	C	P	N	/
Effort:	C	P	N	/

Comments:_____

_____

Study and Work Habits

Stays on Task:	C	P	N	/
Completes Assignments:	C	P	N	/
Works Neatly:	C	P	N	/
Works Independently:	C	P	N	/
Stays Organized:	C	P	N	/

Comments:_____

_____

Recommended Resources*

Special Education, Attention Deficit Disorder (ADD) / Attention Deficit Hyperactivity Disorder (ADHD), and Other Disorders

Atwood, Tony. *Asperger's Syndrome.* Philadelphia, Pa.: Jessica Kinglsley Publishers, 1998.

Brohl, Kathryn. *Working with Traumatized Children: A Handbook for Healing.* Washington, D.C.: Child Welfare League of America.

Goodman, Gretchen. *Inclusive Classrooms from A to Z: A Handbook for Educators.* Columbus, Ohio: Teachers' Publishing Group, 1994.

Irlen, Helen. *Reading by the Colors: Overcoming Dyslexia and Other Reading Disabilities Through the Irlen Method.* Garden City Park, N.Y.: Avery Publishing Group Inc., 1991.

Lang, Greg, and Chris Berberich. *All Children Are Special: Creating an Inclusive Classroom.* York, Maine: Stenhouse Publishers, 1995.

Nowicki, Stephen, and Marshall P. Duke. *Helping the Child Who Doesn't Fit In.* Atlanta, Ga.: Peachtree Publishers, 1992.

Assessment

Bridges, Lois. *Assessment: Continuous Learning.* York, Maine: Stenhouse Publishers, 1995.

Clemmons, J., L. Laase, D. Cooper, N. Areglado, and M. Dill. *Portfolios in the Classroom: A Teacher's Sourcebook.* New York: Scholastic, 1993.

Fiderer, Adele. *35 Rubrics & Checklists to Assess Reading and Writing: Time-Saving Reproducible Forms for Meaningful Assessment.* New York: Scholastic, 1998.

Lazear, David. *Multiple Intelligence Approaches to Assessment: Solving the Assessment Conundrum.* Palatine, Ill.: IRI/Skylight Publishing, 1994.

MacDonald, Sharon. *Portfolio and Its Use: A Road Map for Assessment* (Book II). Little Rock, Ark.: Southern Early Childhood Association, 1996.

Power, Brenda Miller. *Taking Note: Improving Your Observational Notetaking.* York, Maine: Stenhouse Publishers, 1996.

Power, Brenda Miller, and Kelly Chandler. *Well-Chosen Words: Narrative Assessments and Report Card Comments.* York, Maine: Stenhouse Publishers, 1998.

Schipper, Beth, and Joanne Rossi. *Portfolios in the Classroom: Tools for Learning and Instruction.* York, Maine: Stenhouse Publishers, 1997.

Audio/Video

Feldman, Jean. *Fresh Ideas for Active Teaching.* Video. Peterborough, N.H.: Crystal Springs Books, 1997.

Forsten, Char, and Jim Grant. *The Looping Video.* Video. Peterborough, N.H.: Crystal Springs Books, 1998.

Goodman, Gretchen. *Classroom Strategies for "Gray-Area" Children.* Video. Peterborough, N.H.: Crystal Springs Books, 1995.

Grant, Jim. *Do You Know Where Your Child Is?* Video. Rosemont, N.J.: Modern Learning Press, 1985.

——. *Grade Replacement.* Audiotape. Rosemont, N.J.: Modern Learning Press, 1988.

——. *Avoid the Pitfalls of Implementing Multiage Classrooms.* Video. Peterborough, N.H.: Crystal Springs Books, 1995.

——. *Making Informed Decisions About Retention.* Video. Peterborough, N.H.: Crystal Springs Books, 1997.

---

* Many of these titles are available through Crystal Springs Books, 75 Jaffrey Road, PO Box 500, Peterborough, NH 03458. Ph: 1-800-321-0401. Fax: 1-800-337-9929. Internet: www.crystalsprings.com.

Pavelka, Pat. *Creating and Managing Effective Centers and Themes.* Video. Peterborough, N.H.: Crystal Springs Books, 1997.

Classroom Management and Discipline

Albert, Linda. *A Teacher's Guide to Cooperative Discipline.* Circle Pines, Minn.: American Guidance Service, 1989.

Campbell-Rush, Peggy. *Tricks of the Trade In and Out of the Classroom.* Peterborough, N.H.: Crystal Springs Books, 2001.

Cummings, Carol, Ph.D. *The Get-Alongs: A Guide for Teaching Social Skills* (PreK–3). Edmonds, Wash.: Teaching, 1993.

———. *Managing a Diverse Classroom: Practical Ideas for Thematic Units, Reading and Writing, Learning Centers, and Assessments.* Edmonds, Wash.: Teaching, 1995.

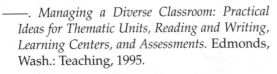

Hollas, Betty. *Improve Student Behavior.* Peterborough, N.H.: Crystal Springs Books, 2001.

———. *Reducing Student Conflict with the Win-Win Way.* Peterborough, N.H.: Crystal Springs Books, 2001.

Nelson, Jane, Lynn Lott, and Stephen Glenn. *Positive Discipline in the Classroom.* Rocklin, Calif.: Prima Publishing, 2000.

Wong, Harry. *The First Days of School: How to Be an Effective Teacher.* Mountain View, Calif.: Harry K. Wong Publications, 1998.

Developmental Education / Readiness

Brazelton, T. Berry. *Touchpoints.* Reading, Mass.: Perseus Books, 1992.

———. *The Irreducible Needs of Children.* Reading, Mass.: Addison-Wesley, 2001.

Grant, Jim. *Struggling Learners: Below Grade or Wrong Grade?* Rosemont, N.J.: Modern Learning Press, 2002.

Grant, Jim, and Bob Johnson. *First Grade Readiness Checklist.* Peterborough, N.H.: Crystal Springs Books, 1997.

———. *Kindergarten Checklist.* Peterborough, N.H.: Crystal Springs Books, 1997.

Grant, Jim, and Margot Azen. *Every Parent's Owner's Manuals.* (Three-, Four-, Five-, Six-, Seven-Year-Old). Rosemont, N.J.: Programs for Education, 1988.

Kraus, Robert. *Leo the Late Bloomer.* New York: Harper-Collins, 1971.

Wood, Chip. *Yardsticks: Children in the Classroom Ages 4–14.* Greenfield, Mass.: Northeast Foundation for Children, 1997.

Differentiated Instruction

Gregory, Gayle H., and Carolyn Chapman. *Differentiated Instructional Strategies.* Thousand Oaks, Calif.: Corwin Press, 2002.

Goodman, Gretchen. *I Can Learn! Strategies and Activities for Gray-Area Children.* Peterborough, N.H.: Crystal Springs Books, 1995.

———. *More I Can Learn!* Peterborough, N.H.: Crystal Springs Books, 1998.

Heacox, Diane. *Differentiating Instruction in the Regular Classroom.* Minneapolis, Minn.: Free Spirit Publishing, 2002.

Tomlinson, Carol Ann, *The Differentiated Classroom: Responding to the Needs of All Learners.* Alexandria, Va.: ASCD, 1999.

———. *Leadership for Differentiating Schools and Classrooms.* Alexandria, Va.: ASCD, 2000.

———. *How to Differentiate Instruction in Mixed-Ability Classrooms.* 2nd . ed. Alexandria, Va.: ASCD, 2001.

Winebrenner, Susan. *Teaching Gifted Kids in the Regular Classroom*. Minneapolis, Minn.: Free Spirit Publishing, 2002.

Grade-Level Retention

Grant, Jim. *Retention and Its Prevention: Making Informed Decisions About Individual Children*. Rosemont, N.J.: Modern Learning Press, 1997.

Grant, Jim, and Irv Richardson. *The Retention/ Promotion Checklist* (K–8). Peterborough, N.H.: Crystal Springs Books, 1998.

Issues in Education

Barrs, Myra, and Sue Pidgeon, eds. *Gender and Reading in Elementary Classrooms*. York, Maine: Stenhouse Publishers, 1994.

Goodman, Kenneth S., ed. *In Defense of Good Teaching: What Teachers Need to Know About the "Reading Wars."* York, Maine: Stenhouse Publishers, 1998.

Payne, Ruby, *Poverty: A Framework for Understanding and Working with Students and Adults from Poverty*, Baytown, Tex.: RFT Publishing, 1998.

U.S. Department of Education. *Prisoners of Time: Too Much to Teach, Not Enough Time to Teach It*. Peterborough, N.H., Crystal Springs Books, 2000.

Wortman, Robert. *Administrators Supporting School Change*. York, Maine: Stenhouse Publishers, 1995.

Language Arts: Bilingual

Samway, Katharine Davies, and Gail Whang. *Literature Study Circles in a Multicultural Classroom*. York, Maine: Stenhouse Publishers, 1996.

Learning Centers

Allen, Irene, and Susan Peery. *Literacy Centers: What Your Other Kids Do During Guided Reading Groups*. Cypress, Calif.: Creative Teaching Press, 2000.

Butt, Donna Sabino, and Kathy Barlow Thurman. *Hey! I Can Read This: The Interactive Book Experience*. Peterborough, N.H.: Crystal Springs Books, 2001.

Cummings, Carol, Ph.D. *Managing a Diverse Classroom: Practical Ideas for Thematic Units, Reading and Writing, Learning Centers, and Assessments*. Edmonds, Wash.: Teaching, 1995.

Feldman, Jean. *Transition Time: Let's Do Something Different!* Beltsville, Md.: Gryphon House, 1995.

——. *Wonderful Rooms Where Children Can Bloom!* Peterborough, N.H.: Crystal Springs Books, 1997.

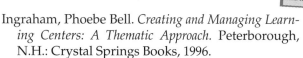

Finney, Susan. *Keep the Rest of the Class Reading and Writing . . . While You Teach Small Groups*. New York: Scholastic, 2000.

Ingraham, Phoebe Bell. *Creating and Managing Learning Centers: A Thematic Approach*. Peterborough, N.H.: Crystal Springs Books, 1996.

MacDonald, Sharon. *Squish, Sort, Paint and Build: Over 200 Easy Learning Center Activities*. Beltsville, Md.: Gryphon House, 1996.

Marriott, Donna. *What Are the Other Kids Doing . . . While You Teach Small Groups*. Cypress, Calif.: Creative Teaching Press, 1997.

Morrow, Lesley Mandel. *The Literacy Center: Contexts for Reading and Writing*. York, Maine: Stenhouse, 1997.

Learning Strategies/Multiple Intelligences

Armstrong, Thomas. *Multiple Intelligences in the Classroom*. Alexandria, Va.: ASCD, 1994.

Campbell, Linda, Bruce Campbell, and Dee Dickinson. *Teaching and Learning Through Multiple Intelligences*. Needham Heights, Mass.: Allyn & Bacon, 1991.

Campbell-Rush, Peggy. *I Teach Kindergarten: A Treasure Chest of Teaching Wisdom*. Peterborough, N.H.: Crystal Springs Books, 2000.

Carriero, Paul. *Tales of Thinking: Multiple Intelligences in the Classroom.* York, Maine: Stenhouse Publishers, 1998.

Gardner, Howard. *Frames of Mind: The Theory of Multiple Intelligences.* New York: Basic Books, 1985.

——. *Multiple Intelligences: The Theory in Practice.* New York: Basic Books, 1990.

——. *The Unschooled Mind: How Children Think and How Schools Should Teach.* New York: Basic Books, 1990.

Grant, Janet Millar. *Shake, Rattle and Learn: Classroom-Tested Ideas That Use Movement for Active Learning.* York, Maine: Stenhouse Publishers, 1995.

Jensen, Eric. *Super Teaching*, Turning Point. San Diego, Calif.: The Brain Store, 1995.

——. *Brain Compatible Strategies, Turning Point.* San Diego, Calif.: The Brain Store, 1998.

——. *Introduction to Brain-Compatible Learning.* San Diego, Calif.: The Brain Store, 1998.

——. *Teaching with the Brain in Mind* (K–6). Alexandria, Va.: ASCD, 1998.

Lazear, David. *Seven Ways of Knowing: Teaching for Multiple Intelligences.* Palatine, Ill. IRI/Skylight Publishing, 1991.

——. *Seven Ways of Teaching: The Artistry of Teaching with Multiple Intelligences.* Palatine, Ill.: IRI/Skylight Publishing, 1991.

——. *Multiple Intelligence Approaches to Assessment: Solving the Assessment Conundrum.* Tucson, Ariz.: Zephyr Press, 1994.

——. *Seven Pathways of Learning: Teaching Students and Parents About Multiple Intelligences.* Tucson, Ariz.: Zephyr Press, 1994.

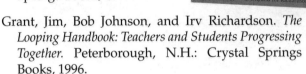

Pavelka, Patricia. *Create Independent Learners* (1–5). Peterborough, N.H.: Crystal Springs Books, 1999.

Payne, Ruby K, Ph.D. *Poverty: A Framework for Understanding and Working with Students and Adults from Poverty.* Baytown, Tex.: RFT Publishing, 1995.

Short, Kathy G., Jean Schroder, Julie Laird, Gloria Kauffman, Margaret J. Ferguson, and Kathleen Marie Crawford. *Learning Together Through Inquiry: From Columbus to Integrated Curriculum.* York, Maine: Stenhouse, 1996.

Thompson, Ellen. *I Teach First Grade: A Treasure Chest of Teaching Wisdom.* Peterborough, N.H.: Crystal Springs Books, 2001.

Wolfe, Pat, Ph.D. *Brain Matters: Translating Brain Research Into Classroom Practice.* Alexandria, Va.: ASCD, 1996.

Looping

Forsten, Char. *The Multiyear Lesson Plan Book.* Peterborough, N.H.: Crystal Springs Books, 1996.

Forsten, Char, Jim Grant, Bob Johnson, and Irv Richardson. *Looping Q&A: 72 Practical Answers to Your Most Pressing Questions.* Peterborough, N.H.: Crystal Springs Books, 1997.

Forsten, Char, Jim Grant, and Irv Richardson. *The Looping Evaluation Book* (K–6). Peterborough, N.H.: Crystal Springs Books, 1999.

Grant, Jim, Bob Johnson, and Irv Richardson. *The Looping Handbook: Teachers and Students Progressing Together.* Peterborough, N.H.: Crystal Springs Books, 1996.

Math

Bamberger, Honi. *Logic Posters, Problems and Puzzles* (3–6). Jefferson City, Mo.: Scholastic Professional Books, 1998.

Barton, Mary Lee, and Clare Heidema. *Teaching Reading in Mathematics.* Aurora, Calif.: McRel, 2000.

Brumbaugh, Allyne. *Big Magic Number Puzzles.* New York: Scholastic, 1992.

Coates, Grace Davila, and Jean Kerr Stenmark. *Family Math for Young Children.* Berkeley, Calif.: Lawrence Hall of Science, University of California at Berkeley, 1997.

Crooks, Lisa. *Munchable Math.* Huntington Beach, Calif.: Creative Teaching Press, 2000.

Currah, Joanne et al. *All Hands on Deck.* Edmonton, Alberta: Box Cars and One-Eyed Jacks, 1997.

Goldish, Meish. *Making Multiplication Easy.* New York: Scholastic, 1991.

Goodnow, Judy et al. The Problem Solver Series and Materials (Grades 1–8). Bothell, Wa.: Creative Publications, 1988.

Lee, Martin, and Marcia Miller. *Great Graphing.* New York: Scholastic, 1993.

——. *Real-Life Math Investigations: 20 Activities That Help Students Apply Mathematical Thinking to Real-Life Situations.* New York: Scholastic, 1997.

——. *5-Minute Math Problem of the Day.* New York: Scholastic, 2000.

Long, Lynette. *Marvelous Multiplication.* New York: John Wiley and Sons, 2000.

Miller, Marcia, and Martin Lee. *Every-Day-of-the-School-Year Math Problems* (3–6). Jefferson City, Mo.: Scholastic Professional Books, 1998.

Pappas, Theoni. *Fractals, Googols, and Other Mathematical Tales.* San Carlos, Calif.: Wide World Publishing, 1993.

Ranucci, E.R., and J.L. Teeters. *Creating Escher-Type Drawings.* Palo Alto, Calif.: Creative Publishing, 1977.

Spann, Mary Beth. *Collaborative Math Books* (K–2). Jefferson City, Mo.: Scholastic Professional Books, 1998.

Stenmark, Jean Kerr; Virginia Thompson; and Ruth Cossey. *Family Math.* Berkeley, Calif.: Lawrence Hall of Science, 1986.

Vydra, Joan, and Jean McCall. *No Problem!* San Luis Obispo, Calif.: Dandy Lion, 1989.

Math-Related Children's Books

Burns, Marilyn. *The Greedy Triangle.* New York: Scholastic, 1994.

De Klerk, Judith. *Illustrated Math Dictionary.* Parsippany, N.J.: Good Year Books, 1999.

Pallotta, Jerry, and Rob Bolster. *The Hershey's Milk Chocolate Fractions Book.* New York: Scholastic, 1999.

Scieszka, Jon, and Lane Smith. *Math Curse.* New York: Viking, 1995.

Viorst, Judith. *Alexander, Who Used to Be Rich Last Sunday.* Fort Worth, Tex.: Aladdin, 1978.

Multiage Education

Forsten, Char, Jim Grant, and Irv Richardson. *The Multiage Evaluation Book* (K–6) Peterborough, N.H.: Crystal Springs Books, 1999.

Grant, Jim, and Bob Johnson. *A Common Sense Guide to Multiage Practices.* Columbus, Ohio: Teachers' Publishing Group, 1995.

Grant, Jim, Bob Johnson, and Irv Richardson. *Multiage Q&A: 101 Practical Answers to Your Most Pressing Questions.* Peterborough, N.H.: Crystal Springs Books, 1995.

——. *Our Best Advice: The Multiage Problem Solving Handbook.* Peterborough, N.H.: Crystal Springs Books, 1996.

Grant, Jim, and Irv Richardson, comps. *Multiage Handbook: A Comprehensive Resource for Multiage Practices.* Peterborough, N.H.: Crystal Springs Books, 1996.

Politano, Colleen, and Anne Davies. *Multi-Age and More*. Winnipeg, Manitoba: Peguis Publishers, 1994.

Stone, Sandra J. *Creating the Multiage Classroom*. Indianapolis, Ind.: Addison Wesley Longman, 1995.

Parent Involvement/Resources for Parents

Chambers, Aidan. *The Reading Environment: How Adults Help Children Enjoy Books*. York, Maine: Stenhouse Publishers, 1996.

Fassler, David, and Lynne S. Dumas. *"Help Me, I'm Sad."* New York: Putnam Penguin, 1997.

Summer Bridge Series (Pre–K, K–K, K–1, 1–2, 2–3, 3–4). Salt Lake City, Utah: Rainbow Bridge Publishing.

Vopat, James. *The Parent Project: A Workshop Approach to Parent Involvement*. York, Maine: Stenhouse Publishers, 1994.

Reading, Writing, Spelling, and Vocabulary

Allen, Janet. *Words, Words, Words*. Portland, Maine: Stenhouse Publishers, 1999.

———. *Yellow Brick Roads*. Portland, Maine: Stenhouse Publishers, 2000.

Allen, Margaret. *The Dr. Maggie Classroom Phonics Kit*. Cypress, Calif.: Creative Teaching Press, 1999.

———. *Dr. Maggie's Phonics Readers: A New View for PreK–2*. Cypress, Calif.: Creative Teaching Press, 1999.

———. *Dr. Maggie's Phonics Resource Guide* (PreK–2). Cypress, Calif.: Creative Teaching Press, 1999.

Atwell, Nancie. *In the Middle: Writing, Reading, and Learning with Adolescents*. Portsmouth, N.H.: Heinemann, 1987.

———. *Coming to Know: Writing to Learn in the Middle Grades*. Portsmouth, N.H.: Heinemann, 1990.

Bean, Wendy, and Chrystine Bouffler. *Read, Write, Spell*. York, Maine: Stenhouse Publishers, 1997.

Billmeyer, Rachel, and Mary Lee Barton. *Teaching Reading in the Content Areas*. Aurora, Colo.: McRel, 1998.

Blotcher, Wendy. *Success with Sight Words* (1–3). Huntington Beach, Calif.: Creative Teaching Press, 1999.

Buehl, Doug. *Classroom Strategies for Interactive Learning*. Newark, Del.: International Reading Association, 2001.

Carbo, Marie. *What Every Principal Should Know About Teaching Reading: How to Raise Test Scores and Nurture a Love of Reading*. Syosset, N.Y.: National Learning Styles Institute, 1997.

Chambers, Aidan. *Tell Me: Children, Reading and Talk*. York, Maine: Stenhouse Publishers, 1996.

Cunningham, Patricia M., and Dorothy P. Hall. *Making Big Words: Multilevel, Hands-On Spelling and Phonics Activities* (Grades 3–6). Torrance, Calif.: Good Apple, 1994.

Daniels, Harvey. *Literature Circles: Voice and Choice in the Student-Centered Classroom*. York, Maine: Stenhouse Publishers, 1994.

Daniels, Harvey, and Marilyn Bizar. *Methods That Matter: Six Structures for Best Practice Classrooms*. York, Maine: Stenhouse Publishers, 1998.

Dorn, Linda J., Cathy French, and Tammy Jones. *Apprenticeship in Literature: Transitions Across Reading and Writing*. York, Maine: Stenhouse Publishers, 1998.

Drapeau, Patti. *Great Teaching with Graphic Organizers* (2–4). Jefferson City, Mo.: Scholastic Professional Books, 1998.

Feldman, Jean. *Ready, Set, Read!* (K–1). Peterborough, N.H.: Crystal Springs Books, 1999.

Fiderer, Adele. *Teaching Writing: A Workshop Approach*. New York: Scholastic, 1993.

Fitzpatrick, Jo. *Solving Writing Problems* (2–4). Huntington Beach, Calif.: Creative Teaching Press, 1999.

——. *Teaching Beginning Writing* (K–2). Huntington Beach, Calif.: Creative Teaching Press, 1999.

Fountas, Irene C., and Gay Su Pinnell. *Guided Reading: Good First Teaching for All Children.* Portsmouth, N.H.: Heinemann, 1996.

——. *Matching Books to Readers: Using Leveled Books in Guided Reading* (K–3). Portsmouth, N.H.: Heinemann, 1999.

——. *Guiding Readers and Writers.* Portsmouth, N.H.: Heinemann, 2001.

Fry, Edward, Ph.D. *1000 Instant Words.* Laguna Beach, Calif.: Laguna Beach Educational Books, 1994.

——. *Dr. Fry's Phonics: Onset and Rime Word Lists.* Laguna Beach, Calif.: Laguna Beach Educational Books, 1994.

——. *How to Teach Reading.* Laguna Beach, Calif.: Laguna Beach Educational Books, 1995.

Haack, Pam, and Cynthia Merrilees. *Write on Target.* Peterborough, N.H.: The Society For Developmental Education, 1991.

Harvey, Stephanie. *Nonfiction Matters: Reading, Writing, and Research in Grades 3–8.* York, Maine: Stenhouse Publishers, 1998.

Harvey, Stephanie, and Anne Goudvis. *Strategies That Work.* Portland, Maine: Stenhouse Publishers, 2000.

Heller, Ruth. *Kites Sail High: And Other Books on Nouns, Adjectives, and Adverbs.* New York: Paper Star, 1998.

Hong, Min, and Patsy Stafford. *Spelling Strategies That Work: Practical Ways to Motivate Students to Become Successful Spellers.* New York: Scholastic, 1997.

Hoyt, Linda. *Revisit, Reflect, Retell: Strategies for Improving Reading Comprehension* (K–5). Portsmouth, N.H.: Heinemann, 1999.

Irvin, Judith. *Reading and the Middle School Student.* Boston: Allyn and Bacon, 1998.

Keene, Ellin, and Susan Zimmerman. *Mosaic of Thought.* Portsmouth, N.H.: Heinemann, 1997.

Krensky, Stephen. *Write Away! One Author's Favorite Activities That Help Ordinary Writers Become Extraordinary Writers* (Grades 3–6). New York: Scholastic, 1998.

Lapin, Gloria. *Sight Word Stories: Alternate Strategies for Emergent Readers.* Torrance, Calif.: Fearon Teacher Aids, 1997.

Lynch, Judy. *Easy Learning for Teaching Word Families* (K–2). Jefferson City, Mo:. Scholastic Professional Books, 1998.

Mader, Carol. *Vowels: Phonics Without Worksheets* Huntington Beach, Calif.: Creative Teaching Press, 1999.

Marzano, Robert, Debra J. Pickering, and Jane Pollack. *Classroom Instruction That Works: Research Based Strategies for Increasing Student Achievement.* Alexandria, Va.: ASCD, 2001.

McCarthy, Tara. *Descriptive Writing.* New York: Scholastic, 1998.

——. *Expository Writing.* New York: Scholastic, 1998.

——. *Narrative Writing* (Grades 4–8). New York: Scholastic, 1998.

——. *Persuasive Writing* (Grades 4–8). New York: Scholastic, 1998.

Moen, Christine. *25 Reproducible Literature Circle Role Sheets.* Jefferson City, Mo.: Scholastic Professional Books, 1998.

——. *20 Reproducible Literature Circle Role Sheets.* Jefferson City, Mo.: Scholastic Professional Books, 2000.

Nickelsen, LeAnn. *Quick Activities to Build a Very Voluminous Vocabulary* (4–8). Jefferson City, Mo.: Scholastic Professional Books, 1998.

Northern Nevada Writing Project Teacher-Researcher Group. *Team Teaching*. York, Maine: Stenhouse, 1996.

Ohanian, Susan. *145 Wonderful Writing Prompts from Favorite Literature* (4–8). Jefferson City, Mo.: Scholastic Professional Books, 1998.

Opitz, Michael. *Flexible Grouping in Reading*. New York: Scholastic, 1998.

Opitz, Michael, and Timothy Rasinski. *Good-Bye Round Robin: 25 Effective Oral Reading Strategies* (K–5). Portsmouth, N.H.: Heinemann, 1998.

Pavelka, Patricia. *Making the Connection: Learning Skills Through Literature* (K–2). Peterborough, N.H.: Crystal Springs Books, 1995.

———. *Making the Connection: Learning Skills Through Literature* (3–6). Peterborough, N.H.: Crystal Springs Books, 1997.

Raphael, Taffy. "Question-Answer Strategy for Children." *The Reading Teacher* 36 (1982): 303-311.

Samway, Katherine Davies, and Gail Whang. *Literature Circles in a Multicultural Classroom*. York, Maine: Stenhouse Publishers, 1996.

Schell, Leo. *How to Create an Independent Reading Program*. New York: Scholastic, 1991.

———. *Building Literacy with Interactive Charts*. New York: Scholastic, 1991.

Scholastic Guide to Balanced Reading: Making It Work for You (Grades 3–6). New York: Scholastic, 1993.

Span, Mary Beth. *26 Interactive Alphabet Mini-Books: Easy-to-Make Reproducible Books That Promote Literacy*. New York: Scholastic, 1997.

Stephens, Elaine C., and Jean E. Brown. *A Handbook of Content Literacy Strategies: 75 Practical Reading and Writing Ideas*. Norwood, Mass: Christopher Gordon Publishers, 2000.

Stitt, Neil. *Take Any Book: Hundreds of Activities to Develop Basic Learning Skills Using Any Book*. Torrance, Calif.: Fearon Teacher Aids: 1998.

Szymusiak, Karen, and Franki Sibberson. *Beyond Leveled Books: Supporting Transitional Readers in Grades 2–5*. Portland, Maine: Stenhouse Publishers, 2001.

Tarlow, Ellen. *Teaching Story Elements with Favorite Books: Creative and Engaging Activities to Explore Character, Plot, Setting, and Themes That Work with Any Book!* New York: Scholastic, 1998.

Trisler, Alana, and Patrice Cardiel. *My Word Book*. Rosemont, N.J.: Modern Learning Press, 1994.

———. *Words I Use When I Write*. Rosemont, N.J.: Modern Learning Press, 1989.

———. *More Words I Use When I Write*. Rosemont, N.J.: Modern Learning Press, 1990.

Tovani, Cris. *I Read It, but I Don't Get It*. Portland, Maine: Stenhouse Publishers, 2000.

Wagstaff, Janiel. *Phonics That Work! New Strategies for the Reading/Writing Classroom*. New York: Scholastic, 1995.

Wittels, Harriet, and Jean Greisman. *How to Spell It*. New York: Scholastic, 1973.

Wood, Karen D., and Thomas S. Dickerson. *Promoting Literacy in Grades 4–9*. Boston: Allyn and Bacon, 2000.

Zgonc, Yvette. *Sounds in Action*. Peterborough, N.H.: Crystal Springs Books, 2000.

Social Studies and Science

Brainard, Audrey, and Denise H. Wrubel. *Literature-Based Science Activities: An Integrated Approach*. New York: Scholastic, 1993.

Edinger, Monica, and Stephanie Fins. *Far Away and Long Ago: Young Historians in the Classroom.* York, Maine: Stenhouse Publishers, 1998.

Julio, Susan. *Great Map Mysteries: 18 Stories and Maps to Build Geography and Map Skills* (Grades 3–6). New York: Scholastic, 1997.

Katz, Bobbi. *American History Poems.* New York: Scholastic, 1998.

Kohl, MaryAnn, and Jean Potter. *Science Arts: Discovering Science Through Art Experiences.* Bellingham, Wash.: Bright Ring Publishing, 1993.

MacDonald, Sharon. *Everyday Discoveries: Amazingly Easy Science and Math Using Stuff You Already Have.* Beltsville, Md.: Gryphon House, 1998.

Ruef, Kerry. *The Private Eye. Looking/Thinking by Analogy: A Guide to Developing the Interdisciplinary Mind.* Seattle, Wash.: The Private Eye Project, 1992.

Steffey, Stephanie, and Wendy J. Hood, eds. *If This Is Social Studies, Why Isn't It Boring?* York, Maine: Stenhouse Publishers, 1994.

Tamblyn, Catherine. *Mega-Fun Map Skills* (K–1). Jefferson City, Mo.: Scholastic Professional Books, 1998.

——. *Mega-Fun Map Skills* (2–3). Jefferson City, Mo.: Scholastic Professional Books, 1998.

Tracking/Untracking

George, Paul. *How to Untrack Your School.* Alexandria, Va.: Association for Supervision and Curriculum Development, 1992.

Kohn, Alfie. *No Contest: The Case Against Competition.* Boston, Mass.: Houghton Mifflin, 1992.

Kozol, Jonathan. *Savage Inequalities: Children in America's Schools.* New York: Crown, 1991.

Oakes, Jeannie. *Keeping Track: How Schools Structure Equality.* New Haven, Ct.: Yale University Press, 1985.

Wheelock, Anne. *Crossing the Tracks: How "Untracking" Can Save America's Schools.* New York: New Press, 1992.

Timely Books for Educators

Bloch, Douglas. *Positive Self-Talk for Children.* New York: Bantam Books, 1993.

Dakos, Kalli. *Don't Read This Book, Whatever You Do!* New York: Simon and Schuster, 1993.

Grant, Jim, and Irv Richardson. *What Teachers Do When No One Is Looking.* Peterborough, N.H.: Crystal Springs Books, 1997.

——. *What Principals Do When No One Is Looking.* Peterborough, N.H.: Crystal Springs Books, 1998.

——. *What Secretaries Do When No One Is Looking.* Peterborough, N.H.: Crystal Springs Books, 1998.

Grant, Jim, and Char Forsten. *If You're Riding a Horse and It Dies, Get Off.* Peterborough, N.H.: Crystal Springs Books, 1999.

Ohanian, Susan. *Ask Ms. Class.* Portland, Maine: Stenhouse Publishers, 1996.

Reavis, George. *The Animal School.* Peterborough, N.H.: Crystal Springs Books, 1999.

Recommended Web Sites

Ask Eric Virtual Library: http://askeric.org/

Crystal Springs Books: www.crystalsprings.com

Interact: www.interact-simulations.com

Staff Development for Educators: www.sde.com

U. S. Department of Education: http://www.ed.gov/pubs/pubdb.html

Yahoo! Reference: www.yahoo.com/reference

www.readinglady.com

www.teachernet.com

www.teachnet.com

www.saxon.com

www.ti.com

To Find Information on Left-Handed Materials

www.thelefthand.com

www.io.com/~cortese/left/southpaw.html

www.anythingleft-handed.co.uk

Publishers and Distributors of Recommended Math Books and Products

Creative Publishing
5623 W 115th Street
Alsip, IL 60803
800-624-0822

Crystal Springs Books
75 Jaffrey Road, PO Box 500
Peterborough, NH 03458-0500
800-321-0401
www.crystalsprings.com

Cuisenaire
PO Box 5040
White Plains, NY 10602-5040
877-411-2761

Dale Seymour Publications
299 Jefferson Road
Parsippany, NJ 07054
800-321-3106

Dandy Lion Publications
3563-L Sueldo
San Luis Opispo, CA 93401
800-776-8032

Interact
1914 Palomar Oaks Way, Suite 150
Carlsbad, CA 92008
800-359-0961
www.interact-simulations.com

National Council of Teachers of Mathematics
1906 Association Drive
Reston, VA 20191-9988
www.nctm.org

Singapore Math
19363 Willamette Dr. #237
West Linn, OR 97068
Ph: 503-727-5473
Fax: 503-722-5671
www.singaporemath.com

Sopris West
1140 Boston Avenue
Longmont, CO 80501
800-547-6747

Crystal Springs BOOKS Call for Writers!

Strategy Proposals

Have you ever wanted to contribute to the creation of a book! Well, here's your chance!

Teachers are always looking for effective, practical, unique, and easy-to-implement curriculum- and classroom-management-related strategies that they can immediately use with their students.

Resources like *Differentiated Instruction: Different Strategies for Different Learners* offers just these "kid-tested" strategies—a perfect resource for the busy classroom teacher.

All of our books have been written or compiled by educators—classroom teachers who, like you, differentiate their instruction in order to meet the needs of *all* their learners. If you have a strategy you would like to share with Crystal Springs Books for a future book project, please submit a brief written proposal following these seven easy steps:

1. Number of words: 300 or less

2. Strategy title: You may include a title for your strategy (e.g., "The Classroom Buzz").

3. Topic: If your strategy is curriculum-related, please indicate the appropriate curriculum area (e.g., math, science, reading, writing). If your strategy belongs under another

heading (e.g., classroom management), please indicate.

4. Grade: Include the appropriate grade/grade-span to which this strategy applies.

5. Materials: If your idea includes materials/recommended resources (title, author/s, city where published, publisher, publish date), please list. If the material(s) is specific to a certain company, please list that company's contact information. Verify all spellings and contact information.

6. Graphics: Include, when appropriate, a sketch or photograph that best represents your strategy and how it works.

7. Reproducible/Supplementary appendix page: If your strategy requires a reproducible or a supplementary appendix page, please submit a separate page that includes the necessary information.

Important Notes

• Although ideas are constantly recycled and repackaged (especially in the world of education!), to the best of your knowledge the strategy you are submitting is your original idea written in your own words.

• Due to a variety of reasons, Crystal Springs Books may choose not to include your strategy in an upcoming publication.

• Should we decide to use your strategy in one or more future publications, we will contact you. If you agree, we will include your name as a contributor to the resource in which your strategy appears.

• Crystal Springs Books reserves the right to edit your write-up for

grammar, punctuation errors, and style issues.

Please submit your strategy to one of the addresses below. Be sure to include your contact information: name, home address, school address (if applicable), telephone number, and E-mail address.

E-mail Address:

publishing@crystalsprings.com

*Type these words in the subject line: Differentiated Instruction

Business Address:

Crystal Springs Books
Attn: Publishing Department
75 Jaffrey Rd.
PO Box 500
Peterborough, NH 03458
Fax: (800) 337-9929

Book Proposals

Crystal Springs Books (CSB) is looking for writers!

If you have a book proposal you would like to share with our publishing department, please check out CSB's web site **(www.crystalsprings.com)** for our Writers Guidelines and manuscript submission process. We would be happy to send you a copy of our Guidelines through postal mail.

We look forward to hearing from you!